P9-DVM-960

WITHDRAWN

Straight Talk
About Smoking

Straight Talk
About Smoking

Rachel Kranz

Facts On File, Inc.

Excerpts on pages 28, 29, 30, and 56 are used with permission from *Washington Week in Review* © NETA-TV, Washington, D.C.

Straight Talk About Smoking

Copyright © 1999 by Rachel Kranz

All rights reserved. No part of this book may be reproduced or utilized in any form or by any means, electronic or mechanical, including photocopying, recording, or by any information storage or retrieval systems, without permission in writing from the publisher. For information contact:

Facts On File, Inc.
11 Penn Plaza
New York NY 10001

Library of Congress Cataloging-in-Publication Data

Kranz, Rachel.
Straight talk about smoking / Rachel Kranz.
p. cm.
Includes bibliographical references and index.
Summary: Discusses the social and medical aspects of smoking, its hazards for health, and ways to stop smoking.
ISBN 0-8160-3976-3
1. Youth—Tobacco use—United States—Juvenile literature. 2. Tobacco habit—United States—Juvenile literature. 3. Smoking—United States—Juvenile literature. 4. Youth—Tobacco use—United States—Prevention. [1. Smoking.] I. Title.
HV5745.K73 1999
362.29'6—dc21 99-10354

Facts On File books are available at special discounts when purchased in bulk quantities for businesses, associations, institutions or sales promotions. Please call our Special Sales Department in New York at (212) 967-8800 or (800) 322-8755.

You can find Facts On File on the World Wide Web at
http://www.factsonfile.com

Cover design by Smart Graphics

Printed in the United States of America

MP FOF 10 9 8 7 6 5 4 3 2 1

This book is printed on acid-free paper.

Special thanks to

Max Antonio Casey Mishler, extraordinary teenager

American Lung Association

American Cancer Society

Dave Shields at Americans for Nonsmokers' Rights

Tim Ellis at 800 All News

Tim Cusick

and, always, Nicole Bowen!

The advice and suggestions given in this book are not meant to replace professional medical or psychiatric care. The author and publisher disclaim liability for any loss or risk, personal or otherwise, resulting, directly or indirectly, from the use, application, or interpretation of the contents of this book.

Contents

1

Society and Smoking

Lynette* and Angelica have been best friends for years. They listen to music together, hang out at the mall together, help each other with their homework. Recently, though, there's been one big difference between them—Lynette has started to smoke.

"Angelica, it's really cool," she tells her friend. "You know how I used to have such a terrible time waking up every morning? Let me tell you, cigarettes are better than coffee—they wake you *right* up. And you know what else? When I'm studying, it helps me concentrate better. You should try it—you'd really like it too."

Angelica doesn't know what to do. She trusts Lynette, and besides, she's always thought that the two of them were just alike. She likes the idea of sharing something else with her friend, and she does think that smoking looks extremely cool. On the other hand, Angelica is really into basketball,

---

* All the people in this book referred to by first name only are *composites*—not actual teenagers, but portraits drawn from many different real-life details.

1

and she knows that smoking is supposed to be bad for athletes. Plus, the whole idea of smoking makes her nervous.

"Aren't you worried about what your folks will say?" she asks. "Or getting into trouble at school?"

Lynette just laughs. "*My* folks smoke," she points out. "And have you *smelled* the faculty lounge lately? Plenty of teachers smoke. They just don't want *us* to have any fun."

Clarence has been smoking for 2 years, since he was 14, and he can't imagine life without cigarettes. He's always been shy, but when he's got a cigarette in his hand, he feels much better—it's a lot less awkward standing around smoking than just standing around. Plus, if he wants to get into a conversation with someone, he can offer them a cigarette or ask them for a light. To Clarence, smoking feels like a nice, friendly thing to do.

Then one day, Clarence reads a news story about some people's claims that cigarette companies have targeted young people in general and African-American teenagers in particular as their next generation of customers. "Why should these companies make money off our people?" says a community leader quoted in the story. "They already have billions. They're making money—and we're dying."

Clarence never thought about it like that before. The idea that someone is manipulating him or making money from him makes him really angry. On the other hand, he *really* likes smoking, and he's not sure how he'd get through a party or a date without a cigarette. Besides, he's heard that it's really hard to quit—and the SATs are coming up. This just isn't the time to add more stress to his life.

Vanessa has never smoked and she doesn't want to. But she feels like everywhere she goes, people are smoking, and she's not quite sure how to handle it. At home, both her parents smoke; at school, the bathrooms are always full of smoke; and when she hangs out with her friends, one or two people are sure to light up.

Vanessa is a singer. She takes voice lessons, she's got the lead in the school musical, and she hopes one day to become a big star. She knows that all that smoke is bad for her throat. But her parents have already told her that they'll smoke if they feel like it. ("It relaxes me," her father says. "Good heavens," says her mother. "It's the one thing I have to look forward to at the end of the day!") And Vanessa feels weird telling her friends what to do.

Understanding Smoking

Have you ever heard the story of the blind men and the elephant? None of the men had ever encountered an elephant before, so each one reached out, trying to understand this new creature through the sense of touch. One person, grabbing hold of a tusk, concluded that an elephant had a hard, thin body. Another person, grabbing the tail, decided that the elephant was soft and skinny, like a snake. Yet another got hold of a leg and insisted that elephants are round and thick, like the trunk of a tree. And so it went, each man thinking he could imagine the elephant on the basis of only one of its body parts.

Understanding smoking is a little bit like that. What you conclude depends on whether you're looking at a table of statistics, lighting up your first cigarette of the day, blowing someone else's smoke out of your face, or making a hospital visit to someone dying of lung cancer. How you feel about the problem depends on how much information you have and what kind of information—whether it comes from personal experience, observing your friends and relatives, studying the facts and figures, or finding out about the different arguments that have raged over smoking recently and for centuries into the past.

It seems even harder to think clearly about smoking when you know that pretty much everyone who talks to you about it has an ax to grind. The tobacco companies want to sell you cigarettes; your parents and teachers are probably telling you not to smoke; your friends may be into smoking or dead set against it.

You've probably also noticed that people aren't necessarily consistent on this issue. Tobacco companies say that smoking is bad for kids—but defend their right to sell cigarettes, cigars, and chewing tobacco to adults. Likewise, politicians go on about the dangers of teenage smoking—while giving millions of dollars in subsidies to tobacco farms and accepting millions more in political campaign contributions from tobacco companies. Your own parents may smoke—while telling you that you're not old enough for such a "grown-up" habit.

So the goal of this book isn't to convince you to smoke or not to smoke. You've got enough people in your life trying to do that already.

Nor is the goal to overwhelm you with a truckload of facts and figures (although we will quote statistics from time to time). Isolated facts are usually not that helpful; you've probably noticed by now that pretty much anyone can quote *some* kind of fact or figure to support his or her position, whatever it may be.

Rather, the goal of this book is to help you think about the subject of smoking in a new way. We'll be talking about the *reasons* people smoke, both the reasons that people give and the scientific studies that have been done on how nicotine affects people's feelings, moods, and performance at work. We'll be talking about the ways the tobacco companies affect your life—their role in politics, movies, music, sports—as well as the kinds of advertising and promotion that they pay for, all to get *you* to smoke *their* brand. We'll be talking about what cigarettes, cigars, and chewing tobacco do to your body—what happens physically when you start smoking, keep smoking, and quit smoking. We'll talk about ways of making decisions—to start smoking, *not* to start smoking, or to quit smoking. Finally, we'll talk about some ways that teenagers across the country have taken action on smoking—how they've addressed this issue in their own communities—and some ways that you can take action yourself, if you decide to do so.

A Personal Disclosure

As I thought about writing this book, I realized that if I were reading it myself, I'd want to know first off where the author stood on this issue. So here's a personal disclosure: I myself don't smoke and never have. I'm fairly sensitive to other people's smoke, enough so that if I'm sitting in a restaurant and someone lights up across the room, I usually smell the smoke right away and look around to see where it's coming from.

But I've also always thought that people who smoke *look* really cool, especially in the movies. The image of a glamorous, sophisticated woman leaning against a bar, blowing a thin stream of cigarette smoke into the air, has always seemed like the ultimate sexy image to me, and I've always loved the character in *Casablanca* played by Humphrey Bogart, tough and heroic, *so* in love with Ingrid Bergman, and smoking one cigarette after another. (However, I really *don't* like remembering that he died of throat cancer at the age of 51.)

Also, I have moments of craving a cigarette, which is odd for a nonsmoker. There are times when I take a break from work or walk into a party and think, "*This* would be the perfect time for a cigarette!" I know that if I actually smoked a cigarette, I'd probably get sick, but that doesn't stop me from feeling that it would be a nice thing to have, at that particular moment.

On the other hand, I think it's a problem that cigarettes (and chewing tobacco, cigars, and pipes) kill so many people—and not in fast, easy ways, but after long, slow, lingering illnesses, filled with pain and suffering and astro-nomical hospital bills. I work in theater, and I know lots of actors whose voices just aren't as powerful or as flexible as they should be because of cigarettes, and lots of dancers who smoke to keep their weight down—and pay for it by getting tired and clumsy a lot sooner than their nonsmoking colleagues. (Athletes are probably smarter than actors and dancers in that way, or maybe they have more respect for their bodies, because they just *don't* smoke, although many do something almost as danger-ous, which is chew tobacco.)

It also bothers me that the tobacco companies, with access to all the same scientific studies as the rest of us, continue to make billions of dollars selling cigarettes, which to me seems as though they're profiting off other people's sickness and death. I'm especially disturbed by all the evidence suggesting that they've made special targets of young people, poor people, African Ameri-cans, and Latinos—the very people in our society who have the least access to health care and who are facing so many other stresses and strains. (The tobacco compa-nies, of course, argue about the medical claims against tobacco, and they deny that anything they do is designed to get anybody to smoke. We'll talk more about these debates in Chapter 2.)

So now you know where *I* stand. But now that it's out in the open, I don't think my personal opinion is all that important. What's important is that *you* have all the facts you need, on all sides of the issue, so that you can decide about smoking for yourself. Because as you probably know, no matter how many laws are passed making it illegal for teens to smoke or socking them with heavy fines for smoking (as some states are starting to do), no matter how many times your parents or your teachers or your guidance counselors say, "Don't smoke," the fact remains: If you *want* to smoke, you can probably get cigarettes, and you probably *will* smoke. So in the end, it's up to you. Hopefully, the information in this book will help you make a decision that's good for you.

How Much Do You Know About Smoking?

Now let's go on to clear the air—no pun intended!—with a little quiz.

(If this book does not belong to you, please write your answers on another sheet of paper.)

1. Nicotine—the major active chemical ingredient in tobacco—holds which place on the Centers for Disease Control's list of the world's most addictive substances?
     a. 1st   b. 4th   c. 5th   d. 10th

2. What place does heroin have on the same list?
     a. 1st   b. 4th   c. 5th   d. 10th

3. In the next 24 hours, how many young people in the United States will start smoking?
     a. 1,000   b. 1,500   c. 2,000   d. 3,000

4. How many of these young people will eventually die of smoking-related diseases?
     a. 1,000   b. 1,500   c. 2,000   d. 3,000

5. What percentage of smokers tried their first cigarette before their 18th birthday?
     a. 40%   b. 50%   c. 65%   d. 75%

6. In a 1986 survey, high school seniors were asked whether they would be smoking five years later. What percentage said they would?
     a. 5%   b. 10%   c. 25%   d. 75%

7. According to the 1992 follow-up study, how many of those surveyed in 1986 were actually smoking five years later?
     a. 5%   b. 10%   c. 25%   d. 75%

8. A 1992 Gallup poll asked teen smokers whether, if they had it to do over, they would start smoking

again. What percentage said they would *not* have started smoking?

    a. 5%   b. 15%   c. 50%   d. 70%

9. Nicotine given to cats had the effect of
    a. stimulating them
    b. relaxing them
    c. simultaneously stimulating and relaxing them
    d. making them nauseous

10. Nicotine was once given to elephants in order to
    a. make them more useful in elephant hunts
    b. put them to sleep via animal dart guns
    c. help them lose weight
    d. encourage them to mate

11. Of people who smoke cigarettes, what percentage are able to control their smoking, as opposed to "needing" cigarettes on a regular basis?

    a. 10%   b. 25%   c. 50%   d. 90%

12. Of people who drink alcohol, what percentage are able to control their drinking, as opposed to "needing" alcohol on a regular basis?

    a. 10%   b. 25%   c. 50%   d. 90%

13. In a number of scientific experiments, what emotion did nicotine seem to suppress, or hold down?

    a. sadness   b. fear   c. happiness d. aggression

14. Which of the following was a cigarette advertising slogan aimed at women of the 1920s?
    a. "You've come a long way, baby."
    b. "It's a woman thing."
    c. "Reach for a Lucky instead of a sweet."
    d. "Nice girls *do* smoke!"

15. Relative to white people, African-American rates of lung cancer are
    a. lower   b. higher   c. about the same

16. What proportion of deaths in the United States per year are smoking-related?

    a. 5%   b. 10%   c. 20%   d. 50%

How do you think you did? Did you know as much about smoking as you thought you did? (Maybe you knew *more* than you thought!) Take a look at the answers and find out.

Answers to "How Much Do You Know About Smoking?"

1. Nicotine—the major active chemical ingredient in to-bacco—holds which place on the Centers for Disease Control's list of the world's most addictive substances?

    a. 1st   b. 4th   c. 5th   d. 10th

2. What place does heroin have on the same list?

    a. 1st   b. 4th   **c. 5th**   d. 10th

   That's right. It's no misprint. The Centers for Disease Control and Prevention (CDC) has actually rated nicotine number one on its list of "most addictive substances." Heroin is number five. That means that smokers who are trying to give up cigarettes are fighting a more powerful addiction than heroin addicts (even though the withdrawal symptoms aren't nearly as dramatic).

   Keep that figure in mind as you read through the rest of this quiz—and the rest of this book. Knowing how very hard it is to break free of nicotine once you've gotten used to it helps to explain a lot.

3. In the next 24 hours, how many young people in the United States will start smoking?

    a. 1,000   b. 1,500   c. 2,000   **d. 3,000**

4. How many of these young people will eventually die of smoking-related diseases?

    a. 1,000   b. 1,500   c. 2,000   d. 3,000

   According to a fact sheet put out by the American Lung Association (ALA), 3,000 teenagers start smoking each day. About one-third of these teens will eventually die of smoking-related diseases. Of course, these deaths don't usually happen for a number of years. But once having started smoking, most people find it very difficult to stop. And as the next set of questions shows, most teenagers have very mixed feelings about their own smoking.

5. What percentage of smokers tried their first cigarette before their 18th birthday?

    a. 40%   b. 50%   c. 65%   ***d. 75%***

6. In a 1986 survey, high school seniors were asked whether they would be smoking five years later. What percentage said they would?

    a. 5%   b. 10%   c. 25%   d. 75%

7. According to the 1992 follow-up study, how many of those surveyed in 1986 were actually smoking five years later?

    a. 5%   b. 10%   c. 25%   ***d. 75%***

8. A 1992 Gallup poll asked teen smokers whether, if they had it to do over, they would start smoking again. What percentage said they would *not* have started smoking?

    a. 5%   b. 15%   c. 50%   ***d. 70%***

In other words, teenagers almost always start smoking with the idea that pretty soon they're going to stop—but they don't. (The American Lung Association cites a similar figure: Of the teens who have smoked at least 100 cigarettes in their lifetime, most of them say that they want to quit but can't.) If you consider that according to the CDC, nicotine is more addictive than heroin, that's not surprising. Of course, if you consider that people who start smoking have a one in three chance of dying from it, it's not surprising that most teens who start *want* to quit.

9. Nicotine given to cats had the effect of

    a. stimulating them

    b. relaxing them

    c. ***simultaneously stimulating and relaxing them***

    d. making them nauseous

10. Nicotine was once given to elephants in order to

    a. make them more useful in elephant hunts

b. put them to sleep via animal dart guns

c. help them lose weight

d. encourage them to mate

From a scientific point of view, nicotine is one of the most fascinating drugs there is, because its effects are so complex. As we'll see in Chapter 3, those smokers who say that cigarettes relax them *and* wake them up are supported by lots of scientific research. When University of Arkansas pharmacologist Karl Ginzel gave nicotine to cats, he found that it both relaxed their muscles and made them more alert. In large quantities—such as those used to sedate agitated elephants—nicotine definitely calms you down. Of course, the nicotine required to calm an elephant would "relax" a human system to the point of death. But in the minute quantities found in cigarettes, cigars, and chewing tobacco, nicotine, unlike virtually any other drug, seems to have a double effect.

11. Of people who smoke cigarettes, what percentage are able to control their smoking, as opposed to "necding" cigarettes on a regular basis?

    a. 10%   b. 25%   c. 50%   d. 90%

12. Of people who drink alcohol, what percentage are able to control their drinking, as opposed to "needing" alcohol on a regular basis?

    a. 10%   b. 25%   c. 50%   **d. 90%**

That's right. Although "problem drinkers" may be more dangerous to society than "problem smokers," the fact remains that *most* people who drink don't do so obsessively. That is, their drinking is under their control; they can drink occasionally or in moderation.

That just isn't true for most smokers. Although about 10 percent of those who light up can "take it or leave it alone," the overwhelming majority of smokers don't have that kind of control. Once they start, they seem to need to get nicotine into their systems on a more or less regular basis. (We'll find some reasons why that might be in Chapter 3.)

13. In a number of scientific experiments, what emotion did nicotine seem to suppress, or hold down?

a. sadness   b. fear   c. happiness   ***d. aggression***

There's a lot of controversy about existing studies of nicotine and its effects on the human body. (Again, we'll learn more about those studies—and the arguments about them—in Chapter 3.) But many scientists seem to have found that in both human and animal studies, nicotine helped suppress anger, aggression, and hostility. Science writer David Krogh, in his book *Smoking: The Artificial Passion,* suggests that this is one reason why smoking is so popular: It may help people get through the day on an even keel without interfering with their performance in the way that alcohol, tranquilizers, or some illegal drugs might do. (Of course, if you're an athlete, actor, singer, or dancer, cigarettes *will* interfere with your performance.)

14. Which of the following was a cigarette advertising slogan aimed at women of the 1920s?

a. "You've come a long way, baby."

b. "It's a woman thing."

c. "Reach for a Lucky instead of a sweet."

d. "Nice girls *do* smoke!"

One reason that many people give for smoking is that it helps them control their weight. In our society, girls and women are under a great deal of pressure to stay thin—even, sometimes, at the cost of their health.

There is some evidence that smoking helps people stay thin and that quitting smoking can lead to weight gain, partly because smoking affects the way our bodies metabolize food (more on this in Chapter 3), but also partly because smoking suppresses the appetite. As a result, smoking appeals to many women who are worried about their weight. ("Since nearly ¼ of all adult American women smoke," David Krogh wrote in 1991, "this is not a trivial matter: some 46,000 American women were diagnosed with lung cancer in 1985 and we can expect that 85 percent of those women are dead today.")

In the 1920s, the makers of Lucky Strike were quite open about using this concern to sell cigarettes, so they said it directly: "Reach for a Lucky instead of a sweet." Today, cigarette makers are more subtle. They simply show ultrathin models selling ultraslim cigarettes—and count on you to get the message.

15. Relative to white people, African-American rates of lung cancer are

       a. lower   ***b. higher***   c. about the same

A higher percentage of African-American men smoke (33.9 percent) than do white men (28.0 percent). And although these black male smokers smoke fewer cigarettes in a day than their white counterparts do, they tend to smoke brands that have higher tar and nicotine levels. Some 48,000 African Americans—male and female—die of smoking-related diseases each year, and as we've seen, lung cancer hits a larger portion of African Americans than of whites.

Of course, there are many reasons that people might get lung cancer. But according to the American Lung Association, "Smoking is directly responsible for 87% of all lung cancer in the United States." The association adds, "The tobacco industry has targeted specific racial and ethnic populations in its advertising and promotion—including African Americans." (The tobacco industry has denied these claims. We'll look more closely at the debate in Chapter 2.)

16. What proportion of deaths in the United States per year are smoking-related?

       a. 5%   b. 10%   ***c. 20%***   d. 50%

The figure sounds a bit more dramatic if you say, in the words of the American Lung Association, "smoking is responsible for an estimated one in five U.S. deaths." Here's an even more dramatic way of putting it, from former U.S. surgeon general C. Everett Koop:

> As a public health officer, we look at the bottom line—which is deaths. I think it's important to know that in the U.S. we lose about 350,000 people a year to premature death from

the use of tobacco. That's like 2 jumbo jets crashing and everybody being killed every day.

Actually, when Koop made that statement, the number of deaths from tobacco was lower than it is today. Now he'd have to say that smoking kills nearly half a million Americans—some 430,700 U.S. deaths—each year. Or, as the Coalition for Accountability puts it, "This [number of smoking-related deaths] is . . . more than are killed by all of the following: Alcohol (105,000); Motor Vehicle accidents, including drunk driving (43,500); Homicides (24,000); AIDS (22,500); Illegal drugs (4,500); Fires not caused by cigarettes (4,200)."

How Did We Get Here?

Imagine this scene on your favorite doctor show.

Doctor Smith: It looks bad, nurse. We're going to have to operate.

Nurse Jones: Oh, doctor, I'm so sorry. You look so tense. Would you like a cigarette to help you relax?

Doctor Smith: Yes, thank you, nurse. Why don't you have one too? Let me give you a light.

Sounds farfetched? It probably does to anyone who watched the series of episodes on the 1997–1998 season of the popular doctor show *E.R.* in which quite a different drama was played out: Dr. Mark Green repeatedly tries and fails to give up smoking until an encounter with a man dying of lung cancer—and still smoking—finally gives him the motivation he needs.

But in the 1950s, before the dangers of smoking were so widely known, doctors and other authority figures frequently smoked on television and in the movies. Smoking wasn't exactly associated with health: Athletes were instructed not to smoke, and sociologist and youth worker Mike Males remembers that cigarettes were labeled "coffin nails" when he went to elementary school in the 1950s. But smoking was generally considered an acceptable, even attractive, activity, and some 50 percent of all adults smoked, along with about 40 percent of all teenagers.

Actually, tobacco has been an important part of the U.S. economy since the days of the first colonists. Although native peoples in the Western Hemisphere had long known about tobacco and used it in various forms—usually as part of religious ceremonies—Europeans didn't know about the substance until Christopher Columbus "discovered" it when he reached the Americas in 1492. Other explorers in the service of Spain brought tobacco back from their travels through North and South America. Then in the 17th century, Sir Walter Raleigh had the idea of bringing tobacco back to England from the colony he called Virginia. In fact, comedian Bob Newhart used to do a stand-up routine in which he imagined a phone call between Raleigh and his "boss," the head of the "West Indies Company," with Raleigh explaining his new discovery. Newhart portrayed the boss, receiving Raleigh's phone call and learning that you could take the tobacco, shred it up, put it on a piece of paper, and:

> Then what do you do to it, Walt? (Laughs) You set fire to it, Walt? (Laughs) Then what do you do, Walt? You *inhale the smoke*. You know, Walt, it seems, off-hand, like you could stand in front of your fireplace and have the same thing going for you. . . . I think you're going to have a tough time, ahh, selling people on sticking burning leaves in their mouths.

Of course, Raleigh didn't have such a tough time, as it turned out. John Rolfe (perhaps best known for marrying Pocohantas) had planted tobacco seed from South America in Virginia, and the tobacco trade had begun. Eventually, tobacco was planted in Europe and Africa as well as in other parts of America. By 1575, tobacco was being regularly shipped to Europe from the American colonies, as well as from Cuba, Trinidad, and Venezuela.

In 17th-century Europe, tobacco was smoked mainly in pipes and was seen as a healthful substance that could stop the spread of disease. As a doctor in London put it:

> To cure headache, a green tobacco leaf on the head; for redness of the face, apply the juice or the ointment of the tobacco leaf; for a toothache, tie a tobacco leaf over the aching region; for a cough, boil the leaves and shake the syrup on the stomach; for stomach pain . . . apply hot tobacco leaves over the region of the belly and re-heat when they get cold.

The same doctor went on to prescribe tobacco in various forms as a cure for cancer, burns, wounds, worms, warts, corns, and bites by a mad dog.

Tobacco soon lost its charm as a European medicine, but smoking continued to be considered a pleasant recreation. Then James I became king of England in 1603. James was one of the first antismoking crusaders. He tried to discourage smoking by raising the import tax on tobacco; soon a pound of tobacco was worth more than a pound of silver. So James tried to limit tobacco imports from Virginia. The result? Farmers in England started to grow their own tobacco, and smugglers started bringing in illegal shipments. James had to accept defeat, so his government—and others in Europe—started a new precedent: They took over the importation and sale of tobacco, making sure that they got handsome tax revenues from sales of the controversial product.

Tobacco continued to be controversial throughout Europe and the United States. As chemists began to study the plant in the 17th century, a sense of its dangers grew. Someone even joked that the following verse should go on a smoker's grave:

> Here lies he who would have lived longer if
> He had not choked himself with a tobacco whiff.

And in 1845, the sixth U.S. president, John Quincy Adams, wrote a letter to Rev. Samuel Cox in Brooklyn, who was in the process of writing a book about tobacco. Adams told Cox that when he was a young man, he had been addicted to both smoking and chewing tobacco. When he decided to quit, it took him three months. He wrote:

> I have often wished that every individual afflicted with this artificial passion could force it upon himself to try but for three months the experiment which I made, sure that it would turn every acre of tobacco land into a wheat field, and add five years to the average of human life.

The next big milestone in tobacco history took place in Raleigh, North Carolina, around the time of the Civil War. In 1856, Abisha Slade invented a special way to cure tobacco that created a bright golden leaf. The smoke from previous types of tobacco had been rough and irritating. It was difficult to draw large quantities of it deep into the lungs and hold it there, and the roughness acted as a kind of natural brake on how much nicotine the body could absorb from a single cigarette. But Slade's new leaf, which was also the result of centuries of breeding tobacco in the sandy soil of North Carolina, produced a much milder smoke. Suddenly, smokers could draw more smoke deep into the lungs, producing a far more satisfying nicotine "hit."

The new product was so addictive that after the Civil War, Northern soldiers often wrote to former Rebel farmers, asking to buy some of "that golden tobacco." Entrepreneur James B. Duke was quick to see the advantages of the new product. "Tobacco is the poor man's luxury," he is supposed to have said. "Where else can he get so much enjoyment for his five or ten cents?" So Duke founded a tobacco company that quickly became one of the largest and most powerful corporations in America, Duke & Sons (later the American Tobacco Company).

For a time, though, Duke's activities were limited because cigarettes still had to be rolled by hand. He brought skilled cigarette rollers—mostly Russian and Polish Jews from New York City—down to North Carolina. He had them teach local African Americans how to roll—and hired the black workers at lower wages.

Then James Bonsack invented the automatic cigarette roller. By 1884, the bugs were out of the system, and Duke's costs for making cigarettes dropped dramatically—from 80¢ to 30¢ per thousand.

Duke understood that the key to expanding the tobacco market was sales. He sent salesmen all over the United States, and eventually, the world, hoping to instill a taste for "American cigarettes" made from the bright leaf tobacco. The company printed colorful ads to announce the coming of a new kind of tobacco, milder and more satisfying than any that the world had ever known before. "We tried to make these advertisements so attractive that people would decorate their homes with them," recalled James A. Thomas, Duke's Far East sales manager.

In the United States, Duke had a host of clever sales schemes as well. He came up with the idea of putting "premium cards"—the ancestors of today's baseball cards—in cigarette packs, hoping to appeal to boys aged 12 and even younger. Unlike cigars and pipes, which tended to make people sick until they got used to them, the new mild cigarettes could be smoked by young people right away, and the cheap price—a pack for a nickel—was something even a child could afford.

Duke created several sets of cards especially intended to attract boys and young men: "Lives of Poor Boys Who Became Rich," "Dangerous Occupations," "Wild Animals," "Beautiful Actresses," and "Sporting Girls." Not only did the cigarette packs come with cards, they also included vouchers. If a consumer sent in enough vouchers, he or she could get a free album for displaying these cards.

Duke created many of the advertising and promotion techniques still used today. For example, he sponsored sporting events. Men and boys were given free cigarettes at the games, while women who attended received cards. Duke also sent people to ports of entry and had them give out free samples to the immigrants entering the United States. He calculated that the free samples were a good investment, since once a person got "hooked" on his gold-leaf tobacco, he or she would be a customer for life.

The consumption of cigarettes grew at a phenomenal rate. In 1885, 1 billion cigarettes a year were smoked in the United States. Only four years later, in 1889, that figure had jumped to over 2 billion, 1 billion of which were sold by Duke. In that year, Duke spent an estimated $1 million on advertising. As John Fahs describes it in *Cigarette Confidential,* "Any surface area that could hold a picture or a brand name was harnessed—calendars, matchboxes, thermometers, rocking chairs—as well as those proto–movie stars, vaudevillians." (Vaudevillians were performers who traveled across the United States, singing and dancing in local theaters. Because they were so famous, Fahs calls them "proto-movie stars," which means "people who created the pattern that movie stars would later follow.")

The 1890s were a time of rapid corporate expansion, but even by the standards of the time, Duke was growing at an extraordinary rate. In those four years, 1885 to 1889, Duke & Sons' worth rose from $250,000 to $7 million. In 1889, Duke acquired four of his largest competitors and formed the American Tobacco Company, which cornered 90 percent of the U.S. cigarette market and had a monopoly on Bonsack's cigarette-rolling machine.

Many members of Congress owned stock in the American Tobacco Company, so they were naturally sympathetic to the fortunes of tobacco. At the same time, however, antismoking groups around the country were attempting to outlaw tobacco sales, sometimes only to young people, sometimes to adults as well. One dramatic moment came in 1905, when Representative Ananias Baker of the Illinois state legislature announced that a tobacco lobbyist had just asked him to vote against a proposed antismoking bill and given him an envelope. Baker opened the envelope right there in front of the crowd—and, in John Fahs's words, "a flurry of bills fell out onto the floor. [T]he [antismoking] bill's fate was sealed." After all, no legislator wanted the public to think that he had voted against the bill because *he* had gotten an envelope full of money!

Early in the 20th century, people began to be concerned about the huge corporations that dominated many parts of the U.S. economy. New *antitrust legislation*—laws to keep any one company from having an unfair monopoly or excess power—led to the breakup of the American Tobacco Company into four smaller corporations: R.J. Reynolds, Liggett & Myers, Lorillard, and a smaller American Tobacco Company. Of the six tobacco companies that dominate the U.S. market today, four come from the 1911 decision that split up James Duke's original company. Today's other two biggies are Philip Morris and Brown and Williamson, which was recently bought by the British American Tobacco Company, or Batco.

Smoking in Our Time

Throughout the first half of the 20th century, U.S. attitudes toward smoking continued to be mixed. On the one hand, smoking was associated with jazz musicians, movie stars, rebels, and outlaws and had an image of being cool, dangerous, sexy, and free spirited. On the other hand, smoking was seen as "American" and acceptable; this was especially true after World War II. Soldiers who came home from World War II and the Korean War were far more addicted to cigarettes than previous generations had been, because tobacco companies had given out free cigarettes at military posts. As we saw, some 40 percent of all teenagers and 50 percent of all adults smoked.

To someone living in today's world—with smoking banned on airplanes and in many restaurants and workplaces; with cigarette advertising banned from television; with nonsmokers becoming increasingly assertive about creating "smoke-free zones"—the smoker's world of the 1950s is almost unimaginable. It truly seemed as though "everybody" smoked (even though only about half the population did).

Then, in 1964, the U.S. surgeon general issued the famous report stating that smoking could be hazardous to a person's health. All of a sudden, the view that smoking was dangerous, even deadly, had a much wider currency.

For a few years after the surgeon general's report, in the late 1960s, smoking rates in the United States actually went up. But starting in the mid-1970s, rates of smoking—especially among teens—began to drop.

Youth worker and sociologist Mike Males believes that teen smoking dropped for two very good reasons. First, adults were getting sick—and the teenagers and young people in their family were watching. Deaths from adult respiratory diseases tripled from 1950 to 1975. Some 2 million smokers died of cancer in the 1970s. As Males puts it, "Glamorous images of smoking media stars of 1955 were replaced by cancerous checkouts among aging notables of 1975."

Second, inspired both by the surgeon general's report and by the evidence of smoking-related diseases, many adults were trying to *quit* smoking, and again, their teenage relatives were right there, watching. Males writes, ". . . an unusually large number of young 1970s adolescents thinking of taking up malignancy sticks were privileged to witness, in their own living rooms, the agony of millions of adult (to wit, their parents) going through the nervous, fumbling, fuming, morosely cursing stopping-and-backsliding ordeal of quitting. Any household who has harbored a quitting smoker knows the enlightening drama these children watched their beloved role models undergo."

The message got through. In 1981, the teen magazine *Senior Scholastic* reported that some 75 percent of the teens polled believed that their peers disapproved of smoking. Between 1975 and 1985, the survey Monitoring the Future found that smoking among high school seniors had dropped by 20 percent, while the National Household Survey on Drug Abuse found that rates had fallen by 40 percent. In other words, 4 million fewer teens were smoking in 1981 than in 1970—and 3 out of 4 who tried smoking did not continue it.

Teen smoking rates continued to fall into the 1990s. By 1994, the percentage of those aged 12–17 who said they had smoked within the past month had fallen to only 10 percent—as compared to 27 percent for those 18–25, and 26 percent for those over the age of 26. Contrary to popular mythology, it seemed that when it came to smoking, teenagers were *more* likely to resist than adults.

Then, in the mid-1990s, the trend started to reverse. Monitoring the Future, for example, found that in 1995, some 31.2 percent of high school seniors reported smoking in the last 30 days, an increase of 12 percent since 1991. The increases were even more dramatic for younger students: 25.4 percent of 10th graders said they had smoked in the past month, up 22 percent since 1991; and 18.6 percent of 8th graders said they had smoked in the past month, up 30 percent since 1991.

A report from the Centers for Disease Control and Prevention (CDC) found similar increases. That report said that 1.3 million people under the age of 18 became daily smokers in 1996, compared with only 708,000 in 1988. The CDC estimates that at least 4.5 million people between the ages of 12 and 17 currently smoke cigarettes. And the CDC said that between 1991 and 1995, the proportion of high school students who smoke had gone up from ¼ to ⅓: Nearly 40 percent of white high school females smoke, and 44 percent of white high school males use tobacco (cigarettes and chewing tobacco). Meanwhile, smoking is also increasing among young African-American males: Between

1991 and 1995, the proportion doubled, rising to 27.8 percent.

The American Lung Association breaks the figures down a little differently. It cites a 1995 national survey of high school students that found that "current cigarette use" was 34.8 percent and "frequent cigarette use" was 16.1 percent.

Teen smoking is important because most smokers start as teenagers. A CDC report found that some 75% of cigarette smokers began smoking before they turned 18. Breaking that figure down further, the CDC interviewed a group of people in their 30s, asking them when they had started smoking. The CDC found that about 15 percent had started at age 11 or earlier; about 21 percent had started at ages 12 or 13; some 25 percent had begun at ages 14 or 15; and around 18 percent had started at ages 16 or 17.

What about other forms of tobacco? The National Center for Chronic Disease Prevention and Health Promotion found in 1997 that 1 out of 4 teenagers aged 14–19 reported having smoked at least 1 cigar in the past year. The ALA cites a similar study from 1996, finding that some 6 million 14- to 19-year-olds, or 26.7 percent of those in the age group, had smoked at least 1 cigar that year.

Smokeless tobacco—also known as chewing tobacco and snuff—used to be relatively rare among teenagers, but its popularity is growing. The Centers for Disease Control and Prevention found that 1 in every 5 males in grades 9 through 12 uses smokeless tobacco. The American Lung Association cites a 1994 survey revealing that 30.7 percent of boys between age 12 and 17 had at least tried some form of smokeless tobacco.

Where Do We Go from Here?

So now you have a sense of the issue: About one-third of teenagers smoke cigarettes, and half of them are already "frequent smokers." Another sizable percentage smoke cigars or chew tobacco.

Of course, lots of adults smoke too. In 1994, some 48 million adults (25 million men and 22.7 million women) in the United States were current smokers. Another way of putting it is the following: 21 percent of all U.S. adults smoked every day, and 4.5 percent smoked on some days, so you could say about $1/4$ of all U.S. adults were smokers.

One of the big changes in the past few years has been the public debate about smoking. Government officials, people from the tobacco industry, and a wide range of health and community organizations have been arguing about smoking and about the responsibility of the tobacco companies. There's also been an intense debate over how to handle both adult and teen smoking. And there's been a huge fight over what types of tobacco advertising and promotion should be permitted.

In order to make your own decisions about smoking, you need to know what these arguments have been about, so we'll look at those in the next chapter.

2

The Tobacco
Debates

Angelica isn't sure how to handle Lynette's smoking. Everything she's read and heard tells her that smoking is bad for you. "If smoking really is bad for my friend," Angelica thinks, "shouldn't I say something to her about it?" On the other hand, Angelica doesn't want to seem like a nag. After all, Lynette's a big girl now. She knows what she's doing, doesn't she?

There's another problem: Angelica really likes the way smoking makes Lynette look. She thinks that cigarettes make her friend look more sexy and confident, more grown up and sure of herself. One day, Angelica and Lynette are having sodas at a coffee shop, and a bunch of older guys from school come in. All of a sudden, Lynette calls over to them, "Hey, who's got a light? I need a light!" The guys laugh and come over and make a big deal about fighting over who gets to light Lynette's cigarette for her. Angelica knows she would *never* be brave enough to do something like that. She starts wondering if cigarettes would make her feel more brave.

Clarence decides he isn't going to quit smoking cold turkey, but maybe he'll cut down. Currently, he's smoking a pack a day. "OK," he thinks, "so I'll just smoke half a pack a day. That shouldn't be too hard. Throughout the day, when I feel like a cigarette, I just won't reach for one right away. I'll wait awhile."

But at the end of his first "cut-down" day, Clarence is surprised to notice that he's only smoked two cigarettes short of a pack. Apparently he wasn't waiting as long as he thought.

The next day, Clarence decides to ration his cigarettes. He'll only smoke 10—that's 1 every hour and a half from 8 A.M. to 10:30 P.M. That doesn't sound too hard. As he lights up his first cigarette of the day, he's sure he can keep to *this* plan without even trying. After all, the first cigarette is always the best. It should be easy to cut back on the rest.

Then, as he waits for the bus to go to school, Clarence starts to get worried that the bus will be late. He *can't* be late today—he has a test first period in math, his hardest subject. Usually, Clarence has a cigarette as he waits for the bus, but now he's going to wait until 9:30, isn't he? If only the bus would come!

Luckily, the bus *does* come, only five minutes late—plenty of time for Clarence to get to school. But Clarence still feels anxious and jumpy, and by now he *really* wants a cigarette. "I can't take a test like this," he thinks. "I'll have a cigarette when I get to school, otherwise I'll fail for sure. I can make it up later in the day."

One day at rehearsal, Vanessa notices that her throat is sore and scratchy. The teacher suggests that she get some cough drops and maybe drink hot tea with lemon and honey when she gets home. Vanessa tries drinking tea, gargling with aspirin dissolved in warm salt water, and using over-the-counter throat spray, but the sore throat doesn't go away. It doesn't hurt *that* much, but it does make Vanessa feel that her singing isn't up to par.

Along with the sore throat, Vanessa starts to notice that she can't hold notes as long as she'd like. Her teacher tells her not to worry, that everybody has ups and downs, and she's sure Vanessa's voice will be fine by opening night. But Vanessa *is* worried. She asks her parents to take her to the doctor, so she can find out how else to take care of her throat and her voice.

The doctor examines Vanessa carefully. Then she asks Vanessa if she smokes. "No," says Vanessa, "I never have."

"Well," says the doctor, "there's nothing wrong with your throat except that it's dried out—the way smokers' throats get dried out. And when you say you can't hold a note, that sounds like shortness of breath—you know, like you can't breathe as deeply as you want to so that you have enough air in your lungs to make the note last."

"Yes," says Vanessa. "That's exactly what it feels like."

"Are you *around* a lot of smoke?" the doctor asks. "Sometimes people have problems with other people's smoke as well as their own. It's called secondhand smoke, or ETS—environmental tobacco smoke."

Vanessa doesn't know what to do. Her house is always full of smoke, and going out with her friends is obviously no escape. But she can't exactly move away from home, and she doesn't want to stop hanging with her friends. Does she have to give up her voice instead?

The Tobacco Wars

What rights do nonsmokers have to protect themselves against *secondhand smoke?* What rights do tobacco companies have to advertise their products? What role, if any, should the government take in controlling when and where people smoke? Should teenagers have the same rights to smoke as adults? Should children?

These are just some of the questions that have driven debates about smoking since 1994, when a number of related controversies about smoking began to make head-lines. As this book goes to press in 1999, most of the issues are not even close to being resolved. Many legal proceed-ings are still before the courts, and several types of legisla-tion are being considered by Congress, state legislatures, and voters deciding on public referendums.

All this activity is taking place against a flurry of news reports about "secret documents" leaked from tobacco companies. To many people, these documents prove that the tobacco companies have repeatedly lied to Congress, tried to manipulate the amount of nicotine in cigarettes in order to get more people "hooked" on smoking, and targeted young people and minorities with special kinds of advertising. The tobacco industry denies these charges.

By the time you read this book, events will almost certainly have moved forward. You'll have to read the end of the story in your daily newspaper—or maybe you'll even take part in creating that ending yourself. Meanwhile, here's the first part of the story, a tale of intrigue, infighting, and court battles that is often complicated but always fascinating.

The FDA Throws Down the Gauntlet

Have you ever heard the expression to "throw down the gauntlet"? A gauntlet is the protective glove that medieval knights used to wear as part of their armor, and when they wanted to challenge another knight to a duel, they literally threw down their gauntlet. Today, the phrase means "to challenge someone, to make the first move."

In 1994, David Kessler, head of the Food and Drug Administration (FDA) from 1990 to 1997, threw down the gauntlet to the tobacco companies. He went to Congress, and in the words of *U.S. News & World Report* journalist Steven Roberts, "his mission was very clear, and that was to convince Congress and the public that the tobacco companies are liars, that they have known all along that the nicotine in their product is addictive and that they have manipulated the contents of cigarettes to enhance that addiction."

Roberts pointed out that "The tobacco companies deny this flat out." But he also explained that Kessler's action had four possible consequences.

1) ***Congress might pass a bill giving the FDA the power to regulate nicotine as though it were a drug.*** Under previous—and current—law, cigarettes are considered neither a food nor a drug. FDA regulations require companies that manufacture food or beverages to list all the ingredients on the label. (You've probably seen those lists of ingredients on the packages of food you've bought.) FDA regulations also stipulate that any drug must be extensively tested before it can be marketed. Among other things, the tests must prove that the drug is not harmful. Based on the tests, the FDA can forbid that a drug be sold or require that it be sold only with a doctor's prescription.

Obviously, if cigarettes are considered neither a food nor a drug, they can be marketed fairly easily. If they're considered a drug, however, the FDA has the power to regulate them or even to require that they be taken off the market altogether. Kessler claimed that because the nicotine in cigarettes is so powerful, it should be considered a drug, and cigarettes should be considered a drug delivery system. (A *drug delivery system* is anything that gets drugs into a person's body. For example, most Tylenol uses tablets as a drug delivery system, though it is possible to buy Tylenol in a liquid solution, which is the preferred delivery system for children. People who have asthma use a delivery system known as an inhaler to sniff their medication.)

Naturally, the cigarette companies want to keep this from happening. They've claimed that the whole idea that nicotine, or cigarettes, are a drug is ridiculous—a ploy by enemies in the government to attack a perfectly legal product that should be available to adults. (Tobacco companies do say that cigarettes should not be sold to minors, people under the legal age of adulthood, which ranges from 18 to 21, depending on the state.)

2) ***There was the possibility that tobacco company executives could be subject to criminal penalties.*** Lying to the public is called fraud. Lying under oath while testifying at a Congressional hearing is called perjury. Cigarette executives had testified at many Congressional hearings that they had not tried to manipulate the levels of nicotine in their cigarettes, that they did not consider nicotine addictive, and that they were not aware of health hazards that might come from smoking cigarettes. Now Kessler was claiming to have documents showing that they had lied.

3) ***More states might sue the tobacco companies to reimburse them for health care monies spent on smoking-related illnesses.*** Florida and Mississippi had already sued tobacco companies for these costs. Kessler's action made it likely that other states would join the first two.

4) ***The tobacco companies were now more open to civil action***. For years, people had been trying to sue cigarette companies, claiming that they had gotten hooked on cigarettes and had then gotten cancer or some other serious disease. No one had ever won such a suit, however. Roberts explained why Kessler's action might make it easier to win one:

> You know, the tobacco companies for years have always won these suits by saying, "Look, people are adults. They can make their own decisions. They're responsible for their actions." But if it can be proven that when those smokers made those decisions, the tobacco companies were being deceitful, then you have the possibility of judges and juries with a very different reaction. It could cost the companies a lot of money.

A Comprehensive Antismoking Bill?

President Bill Clinton was quick to pick up on what Kessler had done. On August 23, 1995, in a Rose Garden address to the nation, he announced his commitment to legislation specifically committed to ending teen smoking.

"Cigarette smoking is the most significant public health problem facing our people," Clinton said. "More Americans die every year from smoking and related diseases than from AIDS, car accidents, murders, suicides, and fires combined."

Clinton went on to criticize tobacco ads:

> Children are bombarded daily by massive marketing campaigns that play on their vulnerabilities, their insecurities, their longings to be something in the world. Joe Camel promises that smoking will make you cool. Virginia Slims models whisper that smoking will help you stay thin. T-shirts and sports sponsorships send the message that healthy and vigorous people smoke and that smoking is fun.

So Clinton called for the tobacco industry to stop marketing and promoting tobacco to children. Specifically, he asked for nationwide public education and a counter-advertising campaign to make smoking seem less glamorous and to provide young people with the facts. He also called for

- mandatory proof of age in order to buy cigarettes
- prohibition of vending machines in areas where children had access to them
- prohibition of advertising near schools, playgrounds, and other places where children congregate
- restriction of outdoor advertisements to black-and-white text—no images permitted

- restriction of advertisements in publications that had a certain percentage of underage readers to black-and-white text with no photographs
- prohibition of targeting children with T-shirts and sports bags featuring cigarette company logos
- prohibition of displaying cigarette or smokeless tobacco brand names at sporting events
- a program of tobacco education for children

Clinton's proposals came under attack from two sides. Tobacco companies thought his plan was an unfair and unconstitutional restriction of their right to free speech. And some antismoking activists thought his plan didn't go far enough.

Compromise and Confrontation

Over the next few years, many changes were made to Clinton's proposal. It eventually took the form of Congressional legislation sponsored by Arizona senator John McCain. McCain worked hard to reach a compromise with the tobacco companies, for he knew that if he could develop a bill that they would support, the bill would be far more likely to pass. If companies opposed the bill, then the companies' many supporters in Congress would perhaps bring the bill down.

In the spring of 1997, the two largest cigarette makers in the United States, Philip Morris and RJR Nabisco (owner of R.J. Reynolds), did in fact sit down with Congress to try to make a deal. Tentatively, the two sides agreed that the tobacco industry would pay up to $300 billion over 25 years into a government fund. Anyone who thought he or she had been harmed by smoking could seek reimbursement from that fund, but not from the tobacco companies themselves.

The compromise was also to include severe restrictions to advertising—not exactly those that President Clinton had proposed, but close. Tobacco companies would no longer be allowed to advertise on outdoor billboards, and their ads couldn't include pictures of actual people, such as the Marlboro man or the Virginia Slims model, though they *could* include cartoons, such as Joe Camel. The manufacture and sale of tobacco products would be regulated by the FDA, as David Kessler had requested, and the companies would share their secret documents with the government.

In exchange, however, the tobacco companies would get full immunity from smoking-related liability. Even if new information came to light from the secret documents, it could not be used by individuals or government groups to sue the tobacco companies. In other words, the tobacco companies would pay now to buy years of safety from further demands or claims against them.

Even as tobacco companies were negotiating with Congress, many of the 50 states were suing the companies, just as Florida and Mississippi had done. States across the nation claimed that they had paid out millions of dollars in Medicaid costs caused by smoking-related illnesses. For a while, the tobacco companies were trying to negotiate with the states as a group to come to a settlement there too.

Part of the tobacco companies' hopes in both cases was to arrange a settlement that would get them permanently off the hook. Their biggest fear was that the national and state governments would come back to them again and again, asking to be reimbursed for funds or passing ever more restrictive legislation. They were also worried about lawsuits from individuals who claimed they had been harmed by smoking. For a time, the companies hoped that by cooperating and compromising, they might end up with legislation and financial settlements that they could live with. They hoped that national legislation would end state suits and civil actions by individuals once and for all.

"This [settlement] gives shareholders and employees more certainty and consumers a respite from constant demonizing of cigarettes," said Martin Broughton, CEO of

British American Tobacco Industries PLC, the group that had bought the American company Brown and Williamson. "They want a big payoff and we want a peaceful life."

"Most important," agreed Steven Goldstone, CEO of R.J. Reynolds, "the agreement secures the tobacco industry's rightful place in the mainstream of legitimate U.S. commerce." Steven Parrish, Philip Morris senior vice president, added, "We hope that . . . legislation will move forward and with it bring a new era of cooperation and tolerance with regard to tobacco issues."

In an editorial in *Tobacco International,* a tobacco industry trade publication, Jane Shea wrote, "Putting an end to the litigation would free the cigarette makers to reassess their business. Initially the settlement would force the companies to make some changes, but throughout its long history the tobacco industry has always been flexible as a rubber band snapping back into shape despite events that have stretched it to the limit."

Then, on April 8, 1998, Steven Goldstone, chairman and chief executive officer of RJR Nabisco, the company that owns R.J. Reynolds, changed his mind. He announced that he and his company were pulling out of the efforts to create a national settlement.

At first, President Clinton and Senator McCain made hopeful statements, saying that they would proceed with their antismoking legislation no matter what the tobacco industry did. But, speaking in an interview on the Public Broadcasting System (PBS) show *Charlie Rose,* tobacco analyst Gary Black said that the company's decision meant the end of legislation. "Without the industry's support," said Black, an analyst at Sanford C. Bernstein & Co., "you're not gonna get the broad advertising restrictions."

By the time the tobacco companies pulled out, the bill also called for a cigarette tax that would have increased the price of cigarettes by $1.10 per pack, a controversial measure. Some analysts said that raising the price of cigarettes was the only proven way to reduce smoking, especially among children and teenagers. Other analysts said that for a tax to have any effect, it would have to be much higher. Still other analysts said that a tax was worse than useless. They pointed out that high cigarette taxes in Canada had led to black-market sales of cheaper cigarettes from Michigan.

In any case, Black's prediction proved to be true. On June 17, 1998, the tobacco bill was defeated. Although McCain, the bill's sponsor, was a Republican, the bill was eventually defeated by fellow Republicans. Both President Clinton, a Democrat, and the Democrats in Congress vowed not to let the idea of antismoking legislation die.

"This bill may be dead," said Senate minority leader Tom Daschle. "But tobacco legislation is not dead. We will not let this issue die. We will come back. We will keep at it."

Suits from the States

As we've seen, the history of the tobacco industry in the mid-1990s is like a rope, made up of many separate strands twisted together. One of those strands was the many lawsuits filed by individual states against various tobacco companies, holding them responsible for medical costs paid by the states to treat illnesses allegedly caused by or related to smoking.

In 1994, tobacco companies had been sued by five states: Florida, Massachusetts, Minnesota, Mississippi, and West Virginia. By 1997, the number had grown to 25. By June 1998, when federal antismoking legislation was defeated, some 40 state cases were pending against tobacco companies, although Florida, Minnesota, Mississippi, and Texas had already settled.

Just as leaders of the tobacco industry had negotiated with members of Congress, so did they meet with a group of state attorneys general. (The attorney general is the head attorney of a state. It is his or her job to take care of the state's legal business. If a state sues a tobacco company, the attorney general is the lawyer in charge of the suit.) Rather than fight each individual case, the tobacco companies wanted to settle with all the states at once. As with the federal legislation, they wanted a deal whereby they would pay some money—perhaps even a great deal of money—in exchange for immunity, the right to be free from future suits by states and individuals.

As with those in Congress, these negotiations with the states were the subject of intense controversy. Some people were thrilled that the states stood to collect funds from the tobacco industry, especially when the industry had settled with Texas for $15.3 billion and with Minnesota for $6.1 billion. Some people thought the states were being too easy on the tobacco industry, because, like the federal compromise proposals, the settlements ended forever all other possibility of collecting from the tobacco companies and, in some cases, forbade the states even to criticize the tobacco industry.

On the other hand, some people thought that the states were, in the words of Jerry Taylor, "pickpocket states," taking advantage of tobacco companies' unpopularity to, basically, steal from them.

Let's look at the arguments a little more closely. Although the state suits differed, they all had one thing in common: They considered the tobacco industry responsible for health problems caused by smoking. When low- and middle-income people covered by Medicaid and Medicare get sick—from smoking-related illnesses or anything else—the states pick up much of the health care cost. The states reasoned that since the tobacco companies had made billions of dollars selling cigarettes and other tobacco products that had made people sick, they should share in paying these costs.

"To this day, despite knowing that tobacco causes cancer and that nicotine is addictive, the tobacco companies continue to mislead the public, withhold what they know and stifle development of safer cigarettes, all the while reaping billions of dollars in profits on their deadly products," said a state of Minnesota press release explaining that state's August 1994 suit.

Jerry Taylor, director of natural resource studies at the conservative Cato Institute, had a different view. He argued that smoking-related illnesses did not in fact cost the state as much money as the state gained in cigarette taxes. He pointed out that in 1994, the state of Florida was spending an annual $290 million on smoking-related illnesses—but gaining $1.9 billion from tobacco taxes, as well as $2.9 billion paid into the state worker compensation fund by tobacco companies.

Taylor also cited figures by W. Kip Viscusi, an economist from Duke University. According to Viscusi, smoking's total cost to society—health care expenses, sick days lost from work, fire costs, life insurance, Social Security taxes not paid (because of lost work time), and the like—amounted to $1.32 for every pack of cigarettes. But, Viscusi said, smokers die earlier in life than other people, so society actually *saves* $1.47 per pack on the cost of nursing homes, pension payments, Social Security benefits, and other insurance costs. After all, if smokers are dead, they aren't using nursing homes or collecting Social Security. So what they cost society in health care expenses and fire damage, they save society by dying early.

Taylor made three other arguments against states collecting health costs from the tobacco companies.

1) Smokers who died from smoking-related illness would not have lived forever; they would have gotten sick and died from *something*—and the state would have had to cover *those* health care costs. So it's unfair to ask the tobacco companies to pick up the tab for people who sooner or later would have gotten sick anyway.

2) The tobacco companies never forced the states to pay for Medicaid or Medicare costs (which were the costs

mentioned in the suits); that's a federal government regulation. If anyone should be sued, Taylor argued, it's Washington.

3) Obesity is responsible for 300,000 deaths per year, and some $70 billion in annual medical costs. Taylor asked, Do the states plan to sue the snack food industry or the people who market meat?

The Tobacco Wars Continue

Because there were so many different suits and so many different back-and-forth arrangements between 1994 and 1999, when this book was going to press, it's not possible to list *all* of the significant state-level events in the tobacco wars. But following are some of the highlights.

- **March 1996:** *For the first time ever, a cigarette company agrees to pay monetary damages for smoking-related illnesses.* The Liggett Group, smallest of the tobacco companies, made a deal with five state attorneys general to pay some $41 million over 25 years. As Betsy Stark, correspondent for the *Wall Street Journal Report* television program, put it, "Perhaps more significant, Liggett has agreed to 'disclose any fraudulent or illegal conduct within the industry.'" Although the Liggett Group's agreement was historic, Stark was quick to note that it would have only a limited effect. Philip Morris, a much bigger tobacco company, announced almost immediately that it would continue to fight suits, rather than settle, saying, "We intend to fight and we intend to win." Stark pointed out that Philip Morris had reason to be optimistic: "After nearly 40 years of litigation, tobacco companies have yet to pay out a dime in compensation. What's more, as a major employer and political contributor, some say the $45 billion industry can expect a certain degree of protection in Washington. Moreover, industry analysts say even if the courts do get tough with tobacco companies, overseas growth will go a long way toward making up the difference." (We'll be talking more about protection in Washington and overseas growth at the end of this chapter.)

- **Early 1998:** *Texas and Minnesota are among the states to settle with the cigarette companies.* Minnesota gets a $6.1 billion settlement; Texas gets $15.3 billion.

- **July 1998:** *The tobacco industry settles suits with 40 states, to pay $368.5 billion over 25 years in exchange for immunity from class actions and punitive damages.* Part of the suit holds that tobacco companies' "secret documents" can remain secret (unlike the Liggett Group's settlement, in which the documents were revealed). Another part of the deal is that nicotine, which former FDA chief David Kessler had wanted to regulate as an addictive drug, will not in fact be regulated. New York state senator Catherine Abate called the arrangement a "sweetheart deal . . . [with] enormous flaws." (A sweetheart deal is when one party lets the other party get away with a lot. Abate was saying that the states had treated the tobacco companies like their "sweetheart," letting them get away with far too much.)

- **September 1998:** *Israel's largest health insurer sues both U.S. and Israeli tobacco companies.* A $2 billion lawsuit is filed against Philip Morris Cos., R.J. Reynolds, Brown & Williamson (owned by the British American Tobacco Company), Liggett & Myers (the Liggett Group), and Lorillard, as well as Dubek, Israel's only cigarette maker.

- **October 1998:** *The first smokers' class-action lawsuit against the tobacco industry begins.* A lawsuit known as *Engle vs. R.J. Reynolds Tobacco Co.* opens in Dade County Circuit Court in Florida. The suit is a class-action suit, which means that it's an action taken on behalf of a whole class, or group, of people. Anyone who fits the definition of the class can join. In this case, the definition is "all Florida residents injured by cigarette smoking and their survivors." Usually, even the biggest class-action lawsuit covers 150,000 to 200,000 people—but this suit might include up to 1 million. The lead plaintiff (person bringing the suit) is Howard Engle, a retired pediatrician who claims that the smoking he began during his first year at medical school eventually caused his asthma. Other claims include those of Frosene D. Steevans, who says that 27 years of smoking forced her to have quadruple heart bypass surgery in 1989; and Raymond Lacey, who said he became addicted to smoking at age 11 and developed a circulatory disease that caused him to have both his legs amputated 12 years ago. The case names R.J. Reynolds, Philip Morris, Brown & Williamson, Lorillard, and Liggett.

- **October 5, 1998:** *Washington State settles out of court with a smokeless tobacco company.* It's not just cigarettes that have come under fire. Smokeless tobacco—chewing tobacco, or snuff—is also considered a health hazard by many who are concerned about its growing popularity among teenage boys. (We'll learn more about the effects of smokeless tobacco in Chapter 3.) Washington State's settlement with UST Inc. and the Smokeless Tobacco Council (a trade group whose purpose is to promote the use of smokeless tobacco) does not net the state a lot of money, but it does win significant concessions from the smokeless tobacco industry. UST Inc. and the council agree to pay $2 million to reimburse the state's legal costs in the suit, discontinue all advertising on billboards and mass transit in Washington, and not to oppose any future state legislation intended to limit tobacco sales.

- **November 1998:** *After one of the closest elections in California history, voters ratify Proposition 10, a proposal to raise the tobacco tax by 50¢ a pack.* "Prop 10," as it was known during the campaign, was a major project of film director and former *All in the Family* star Rob Reiner, who enlisted the support of many

Hollywood stars, including director Steven Spielberg, actor/comedian Robin Williams, and his own father, director/comedian Carl Reiner. Prop 10 will make California the third most expensive state for smokers. The $700 million generated will be used to pay for statewide tobacco education programs and local social services. The vote was extremely close, with just 50.4 percent of voters supporting the controversial measure, which passed by less than 60,000 votes out of some 7.6 million total votes cast. In fact, the vote was so close that Californians had to wait over a week to hear the result—after the absentee ballots (votes that residents had to mail in) had been counted.

- **November 1998: *Forty-six states agree to a $206 billion tobacco settlement.*** The money—considered to cover the health costs of smoking—will be paid out by the tobacco companies over a 25-year period, in order to end lawsuits by the states. In some ways, this is a historic settlement—the largest civil settlement in U.S. history (that is, the largest amount of money ever awarded in a suit). But critics of the tobacco industry claim that the deal does not go nearly far enough. If Congress had passed the deal proposed in 1997, for example, the tobacco companies would have had to pay some $368.5 billion. And the industry would have had to pay further penalties if smoking among young people did not drop. Moreover, the earlier deal would have left the industry under the supervision of the Food and Drug Administration, with the nicotine in tobacco classified as a drug. Unlike the 1997 settlement, the new deal allows retailers to keep advertising cigarettes, does not ban vending machines, lets tobacco companies sponsor sporting events, and does not demand stronger health warnings on cigarette packs. Although it does ban cartoon characters like Joe Camel, it does not prevent the use of glamorous figures such as the Marlboro Man. John R. Garrison, chief executive officer of the American Lung

Association (ALA), says that the ALA is "disappointed" in the deal. "It is not a settlement," says Garrison, quoted in a November 16 bulletin by Reuters news agency, "it is a partnership between the tobacco companies and the [states'] attorneys general that allows Big Tobacco to continue in its nefarious business as usual." "The deal would leave the Marlboro Man in the saddle and the tobacco companies in the driver's seat," says Jeffrey Barg, president of the Coalition for a Tobacco-Free Pennsylvania, as quoted in the *Cincinnati Post* on November 17. The same issue quotes consumer advocate Ralph Nader as saying the arrangement let the industry "get off cheap." "I think this is a very bad deal for California," agrees Professor Stanton Glantz, the man who first exposed the secret "cigarette papers," quoted in the *San Francisco Chronicle* of November 17. (See the next section.) The deal is also opposed by former U.S. surgeon general C. Everett Koop and former FDA chief David Kessler. Meanwhile, class-action suits—brought by individuals who claim that tobacco has damaged their health—continue.

- **1998:** ***Philip Morris Co.'s fourth-quarter profits drop 79 percent, mostly because of how much the settlement cost the company.*** However, if the legal expenses were not figured in, the company's earnings would have risen by 9 percent, thanks to an increase of some 65¢ per pack over 1998. Despite the higher prices, Philip Morris nets a record 56.2 percent of U.S. cigarette sales.

- **January 1999:** ***The Justice Department asks the Supreme Court to overturn a ruling that keeps the FDA from regulating tobacco products, as President Clinton announces in his State of the Union address his commitment to take the tobacco companies to court.*** When the tobacco companies settled with 46 states, most observers believed that the industry's troubles were over. The events of January 1999 show that the federal government is not yet ready to end its battle with cigarette and smokeless tobacco makers. Although tobacco industry officials and some analysts dismissed the threats, some observers pointed out that the president might have an underlying agenda: Roy Burry, a tobacco industry analyst with Brown Brothers Harriman, thinks the lawsuit is the president's way to force tobacco companies to accept a 55¢-a-pack tax on cigarettes.

- **January 1999:** *The Reverend Jesse Brown and associates file a complaint claiming that tobacco companies have illegally targeted African Americans.* The suit, filed in U.S. district court in Pennsylvania, names all the major tobacco companies, the Council for Tobacco Research, the Tobacco Institute, the Smokeless Tobacco Council, and others. It alleges that the industry has "engaged in a conspiracy to conceal from and to mislead and deceive Black Americans" about the dangers of tobacco, and that among other things, it targeted them with regard to menthol cigarettes.

- **February 1999:** *The World Health Organization, an agency of the United Nations, plans to introduce a public health treaty by 2003, banning tobacco advertising and possibly public smoking worldwide.* If this treaty is ratified, it would be the world's first public health treaty.

- **February 1999:** *Canadian provinces join British Columbia in a multibillion-dollar lawsuit against Canadian tobacco manufacturers.* Inspired by news of the U.S. settlement, Canadians join forces to fight their own tobacco industry. "When the news broke out in the States of the billion-dollar reward, it was like a bucket of water on the heads of politicians in Canada," says a British Columbian. "It woke us up to the possibilities here."

As we said, this story is still being written. Actions taken by adults—and young people—in states around the nation are making a difference as to what kind of policy we'll have about cigarettes, smokeless tobacco, and the tobacco industry. If you'd like to find out the latest, look at your daily newspaper, call one of the groups listed in Chapter 7, or check in regularly with one of the web sites also listed in Chapter 7. There you can find ways to stay informed—and maybe, also, to get involved. (For more about how to get involved on this issue, see Chapter 6.)

The Tobacco Companies' "Secret Documents"

If anybody tells you that some forces are too powerful to fight, that some things don't change, that some battles can't be won, just point to 1994 and the history of the tobacco companies. For years, it was virtually impossible even to imagine taking them to court and winning. Then suddenly, they were deluged with suits, not just from individuals, but from state governments. They were settling out of court for enormous sums, and at press time they had yet to face the Florida class-action suit, the largest class-action case in history. What made the difference? The answer lies in the story of the tobacco industry's secret files.

On May 12, 1994, Professor Stanton Glantz of the University of California, San Francisco (UCSF) received a box of documents dating from the early 1950s to the early 1980s. The return address on the box read only "Mr. Butts." When Professor Glantz opened the box, to his amazement he found hundreds of confidential internal memos from Brown and Williamson and its owner, British American Tobacco.

A few days before, press reports of these documents had started to appear. And when the U.S. House of Representatives' Subcommittee on Health and the Environment held hearings, on June 23, 1994, they had some of the confidential documents too.

The question of where the documents came from has been widely debated and is summarized in a 1996 book entitled *The Cigarette Papers,* by Stanton A. Glantz, John Slade, Lisa A. Bero, Peter Hanauer, and Deborah E. Barnes. We'll be summarizing the high points here, but if you're interested in finding out more, you can look at the book yourself. If you have access to a computer, you can find the electronic version of the book, as well as 8,000 pages of documents, at http://www.library.ucsf.edu/tobacco.

What the documents seemed to reveal was a decades-long pattern of tobacco company misconduct that shocked even public health advocates who had opposed the tobacco companies for years. "I had no idea, no idea that the industry knew these many things about addiction, about how to manipulate nicotine," said Dr. Richard Hurt of the Mayo Clinic in an article in the *Journal of the American Medical Association.* "We had some hints, [but] this goes beyond anybody's wildest dreams about what they knew and when they knew it."

The main revelation of the papers was, as Dr. Hurt suggested, that the tobacco companies seemed to be aware that nicotine was addictive and to use that knowledge to manipulate the nicotine content of their cigarettes and smokeless tobacco. That way, they'd get customers hooked on what, it now appears, even the tobacco companies knew was a deadly habit.

As we saw in Chapter 1, many people, including scientists at the Centers for Disease Control, had claimed that nicotine was an addictive substance and that it was harder to break a nicotine addition than a heroin habit. But for years, the tobacco industry had denied both that nicotine was addictive and that they could control how much nicotine was in a particular cigarette.

The "cigarette papers" suggest otherwise. Dr. Hurt spent weeks studying the secret documents before he and Channing Robertson wrote the *JAMA* article. An article about Hurt's experience, published in the *Minneapolis Star-Tribune,* cited the following quote from the tobacco industry: "It's fortunate that cigarettes are a habit that they can't break." That and other damning quotes certainly make it look as though the tobacco companies *did* know that cigarettes are addictive.

The Association on Smoking and Health (ASH) prepared a summary of the documents. Here's what it found on various points.

- ***Smoking and health:*** Although the industry denied and continues to deny that smoking causes lung cancer, the documents seem to show that in fact, it understands that cigarettes are carcinogenic (cancer-causing)—and that they have understood this since the 1950s.
- ***Nicotine and addiction:*** Although the industry has denied that cigarettes are addictive, it seems that it's been aware of the addictive properties of nicotine since the 1960s.
- ***Marketing to children:*** The industry has repeatedly denied that it targets young people and tries to get them interested in smoking. The documents, however, reveal what many observers had already charged: that without a continuous supply of young smokers, the industry would be in big trouble and that advertising and marketing are geared to reaching the young.
- ***Advertising:*** The industry has long argued that its advertising was aimed at winning over existing smokers to a particular brand, not at convincing nonsmokers to smoke. But, as the ASH puts it, "The documents show that advertising is crucial in nurturing the motivation to smoke by creating or projecting the positive values, such as independence, machismo, glamour or intelligence erroneously [falsely] associated with the product."
- ***Cigarette design:*** As ASH explains, "The documents show that the companies initially hoped to make safer cigarettes, but then abandoned the enterprise when it recognised that this would expose their existing products as 'unsafe.' The industry had deliberately promoted 'low-tar' cigarettes knowing that they would offer false

reassurance without health benefits. [We'll learn more about low-tar cigarettes and why they aren't as healthy as they seem in Chapter 3.] It has manipulated nicotine and introduced additives to change the delivery of nicotine. [In other words, the companies doctored their cigarettes so smokers would get a greater hit of nicotine. We'll talk more about that also in Chapter 3.] It recognizes the cigarette as a drug delivery device."

Another antitobacco group, the Coalition for Accountability, put together its own summaries of tobacco industry misconduct. Following are some quotes that it found within the "tobacco papers."

- "It seems unlikely that we will be able to locate a toxicologist [a scientist who studies poisons] who will give a 'clean' opinion to tobacco, even if (s)he agrees that ingredients pose no risk. The most realistic hope is that we can get an opinion that tobacco is a 'risk factor.'"—1986 R.J. Reynolds (RJR) document.
- "This young adult market, the 14-to-24 age group . . . represent(s) tomorrow's cigarette business."—1974 RJR memo.
- ". . . comic-strip type copy might get a much higher readership among younger people than any other type of copy."—1973 RJR memo.
- "[T]he amount of evidence accumulated to indict [accuse] cigarette smoke as a health hazard is overwhelming. The evidence challenging such an indictment is scant." —1962 RJR memo.
- Cigarettes "cause or predispose, lung cancer . . . They contribute to certain cardiovascular disorders . . . They may well be truly causative in emphysema, etc., etc."—1963 internal memo from Addision Yeaman, executive vice president of Brown and Williamson, president of Council for Tobacco Research

- "Without nicotine . . . there would be no smoking . . ."
  —1972 Philip Morris researcher
- "We are, then, in the business of selling nicotine, an addictive drug . . ." —1963 internal memo from Addison Yeaman, executive vice president of Brown and Williamson, president of Council for Tobacco Research

Finally, the secret documents contain detailed discussion of various ways to create higher-nicotine tobaccos: by adding a chemical known as "Compound W"; by changing cigarette paper; by developing a genetically altered tobacco plant known as Y-1; and by a variety of other means.

Tomorrow's Cigarette Business

As we just saw, one of the key ways that the tobacco industry wanted to grow and expand was by attracting young people, both through advertisements—billboards, magazine ads, names on sports cars, sponsorship of sports events—and through promotions—free items such as gym bags and cigarette lighters bearing a company name and logo.

To understand this process better, let's focus for a moment on the power of advertising. Advertising is such a big part of our daily lives that sometimes it's hard to notice. After all, you see ads on TV, hear ads on the radio, read ads in newspapers and magazines. You may even use material in school that comes from a corporate sponsor—a form of advertising. Or you might watch a sports event, attend a concert, or go to an arts festival that is sponsored by a corporation whose name is part of the event or whose logo appears in the program—yet another kind of advertising. Perhaps you notice the logos on a friend's shoes or see the commercial message on his or her T-shirt or jacket. Can you think of other places where you come into contact with ads?

So one very important question to ask is, How much do you think advertising influences people? How much do you think it influences *you?* If someone told you that your opinions, your thoughts, and even your actions were being swayed by billboards on the street and pictures in magazines, would you be surprised? Insulted? Puzzled?

Ever since the birth of modern advertising in the 1920s, questions about advertising's influence have been the subject of heated public debate. Over the years, some people have argued that advertising affects us very deeply, more than we realize. Others have pooh-poohed this notion, claiming that no matter what images, slogans, and ideas we are presented by TV, radio, outdoor, and print advertising, in the end, we are creatures of free will, and we decide for ourselves.

Still other people have argued a third case. They point out that while of course each individual makes personal decisions about what to do at any given moment, advertising has a powerful impact on the climate within which those decisions are made. People who argue this point of view agree that no one decides to start smoking just because he or she sees a single billboard that portrays a rugged Marlboro man or a glamorous Virginia Slims woman.

On the other hand, they say, viewing image after image, day after day, year after year, adds up to a portrait of, say, smoking as glamorous, widespread, exciting, and, by implication, safe. Imagine, say these critics of the advertising industry, how differently we might all feel about smoking if for every image of a slender, beautiful women holding a cigarette, we also saw the picture of a haggard woman, wrinkled before her time, nicotine stains on her teeth, coughing and spitting. Imagine if for every picture of a rugged cowboy or a clean-cut young man, we also saw an athlete panting and gasping, unable to perform at peak standards because of the effects of cigarettes on the lungs.

Certainly tobacco companies know which side of the debate they're on. They believe so strongly in the power of advertising to affect people's thoughts and actions that in 1993 they spent $6.02 billion trying to get people to buy their cigarettes, according to a 1993 Federal Trade Commission Report to Congress. And, according to Americans for Nonsmokers' Rights, the American Lung Association, and a number of other groups, the tobacco industry is targeting youth, minorities, women, and gays and lesbians.

As far as very young children go, the tobacco industry seems to be getting its message out. As long ago as 1991, "Old Joe," the cartoon camel used by Camel to advertise its cigarettes, was familiar to 91 percent of all 6-year-olds in a study whose results were published in the *Journal of the American Medical Association.* In fact, as many six-year-olds recognized Joe Camel as could recognize the famous cartoon character Mickey Mouse.

Joe Camel's message isn't lost on teenagers either. When the Joe Camel character was first introduced in 1988, only 0.5 percent of the under-18 market bought Camel cigarettes, which were seen as "rough," old fashioned, and not particularly cool. After three years of watching Joe Camel play pool, hang out on street corners, and have fun with his friends, people under 18 seemed to change their mind about the Camel brand. In only 3 years, 32.8 percent of that market—almost a full third—were buying Camel cigarettes.

Here's another statistic that suggests how powerful advertising can be. The three most heavily advertised brands of cigarettes are Marlboro, Camel, and Newport, and these brands are the ones that 86 percent of teen smokers buy, when they buy their own cigarettes. And one more example of the power of advertising: A 1993 national survey found that 35 percent of 12- to 17-year-olds and 50 percent of 18- to 24-year-olds either had a promotional catalog, owned a promotional item, or were saving coupons for premiums given out by the tobacco companies.

A promotional item is an object that a tobacco company gives away or exchanges for one or more coupons that a person gets when he or she buys cigarettes. A promotional catalog lists those promotional items and tells you how to order them. So, for example, a cigarette lighter with a picture of Joe Camel or a key chain with the Marlboro logo on it would be promotional items for Camel or Marlboro cigarettes. You might get those objects for free, or you might need to save up coupons and send them in to get these "free gifts" that are really advertising.

How Does Advertising Affect *You?*

It's hard to admit that we're affected by the images we see and the slogans we hear. But if we are indeed affected, then becoming aware of the power of advertising and its images is the first step to freeing ourselves from that power.

Try this exercise to gauge the power of advertising in your life—and in your world. For one week, notice every time you see an image of smoking. If you can, jot down the "sighting" in a notebook. Note whether you saw a billboard; a magazine ad; a newspaper ad; an image of cigarettes in a movie or TV show; the logo of a cigarette company on a racing car or at another sports event; or a promotional item such as a cigarette lighter, keychain, poster, or matchbook that promotes the use of cigarettes, cigars, or chewing tobacco. Also note whether you've seen images of smoking in ads for other products, such as beer, hard liquor, or restaurants.

Try to note where you saw the image and then add a word or two to describe it. Here's an excerpt from Angelica's log:

Monday: Joe Camel billboard on way to school—"tough," "cool"
Virginia Slims ad in magazine—"glamorous," "free"
Tuesday: TV sitcom, *Where's the Beef?*—"funny," "silly"
Camel matchbook in our kitchen—no image, just there

Marlboro logo on car in Marlboro Grand Prix race—"fast," "winner"

At the end of the week, jot down your quick responses to each of these questions.

- Did I see a few, some, or many images of smoking?
- Did I see more, the same, or fewer images than I expected?
- What was the overall image of smoking that was presented to me?
- What effect did this image have on me?

Now what do you think of the power of advertising? Do you think it affects you a little, somewhat, a lot, or not at all? How do you think it affects other people you know? Even if it doesn't get you to buy a particular product, does it make you feel a certain way about the way you look or the things you own? Does it make you wish for things you don't have, or maybe make you feel like other people are having all the fun and you're left out?

Maybe you're one of those lucky people advertising doesn't affect. But if you *do* discover wishes, fantasies, and longings in yourself that connect to the images you see in ads, take heart—you're not alone. Part of why advertising is so powerful is because it plays on our very deep feelings in ways that we don't even notice. Now that you're more aware, you can start asking questions about the place that advertising can and should have in your life and in your world.

One big part of the debate about tobacco is whether or not cigarettes and other tobacco products should be advertised. Critics of the tobacco industry say that ads get susceptible people, particularly children, to smoke—or at least to be more receptive to smoking. A variety of groups—the tobacco industry, the American Civil Liberties Union (ACLU), a group called the Freedom to Advertise

Coalition, and others—argue that advertising comes under the heading of *free speech* and is therefore guaranteed by the Constitution. Still others argue that advertising is relatively unimportant in the effort to stop smoking—or at least, that it's not the most important factor.

We'll look further at this debate in Chapter 6, where we talk about ways that you can take action to express your ideas about smoking. We'll also talk about other ideas people have put forward to combat smoking, such as high antismoking taxes, fines for young people caught with cigarettes, and punishments for merchants who sell tobacco products to teenagers and children. You'll have a chance to think more about how you feel about smoking and what our society should do about it.

But before you're through with the tobacco debates, there's one more thing you have to know.

Living in a Tobacco Economy

Advertising is only one way that the tobacco industry helps to shape the world we live in. Another very important influence is through its power in the economy. Let's take a closer look at that power and at the many different ways that it affects our political institutions, our foreign relations, and our culture.

The tobacco industry is responsible for some 700,000 jobs. That number represents the people who grow, process, manufacture, distribute, and promote tobacco in all its forms: tobacco farmers, advertising executives, the guy who refills and maintains the cigarette machine, the woman who designs the company logo. To get a full sense of tobacco's role in the economy, though, you'd probably also have to figure in the scientists, doctors, and related professionals who deal with people suffering from smoking-related illnesses; the drug store employees who sell and the factory workers who make nicotine gum, nicotine patches, and other "quit-smoking" devices; and the researchers, analysts, and lawyers who do research, write papers, and go to court over issues related to smoking. Science writer Laurence Pringle has even suggested that we add funeral directors to the part of the economy supported by smoking, since smokers on average die eight years sooner than nonsmokers.

There are six major tobacco companies in the United States, most of which sell other products as well as tobacco. About three-quarters of all tobacco business is done by just two companies: Philip Morris and RJR Nabisco, which owns R.J. Reynolds. Nabisco also makes cookies, cereals, and other foods. Philip Morris owns Kraft General Foods and Miller Beer.

As the industry leader, Philip Morris pays some $4 billion a year in taxes. It also sells $4 billion worth of products overseas, which helps with the United States's balance of payments. (The balance of payments is the relationship between the value of U.S. goods sold overseas and the balance of overseas goods sold in the United States. Economists generally believe that it's better for the U.S. economy if the balance is either equal or in the United States's favor, that is, if the United States sells more goods than it buys.) In fact, expanding markets in Asia and eastern Europe are increasingly important to all of the major tobacco companies.

The United States is the largest exporter in the world of manufactured tobacco products (cigarettes, pipe tobacco, cigars, smokeless tobacco, and the like), and it is almost tied with Brazil as the number-one exporter of unprocessed tobacco leaf (sold to countries who then make their own tobacco products from it). In 1993 the United States exported 458 million pounds of leaf tobacco, at a value of $1.31 billion, primarily to Germany, Japan, and the Netherlands, along with $4.25 billion worth of manufactured tobacco products, mainly to

Japan, Belgium, Luxembourg, Hong Kong, Saudi Arabia, and the United Arab Emirates.

Tobacco is central to the economies of six states: Florida, Georgia, Kentucky, North Carolina, South Carolina, and Virginia. These are the main states that grow and/or process tobacco. In some southern states, more than 20 percent of all agricultural income comes from tobacco. So when you think about tobacco's role in the economy, think of the people in those states who make and sell farm machinery, fertilizer, gasoline, and other equipment needed to farm. Then think of the people who sell food, clothing, and other items to the farmers who grow tobacco. All of these people depend to some extent on tobacco sales for their livelihoods.

The Power of Tobacco

How, then, does this economic power affect our world? Well, first of all, it gives tobacco companies enormous power in the states where tobacco is key to the economy. For example, in 1989 in Kentucky—the nation's leading tobacco grower and the state with the most smoking-related deaths—the University of Louisville instituted some new restrictions on smokers. The university, a public institution, is funded by the state legislature, and the legislature threatened to cut the university's budget if it did not weaken the restrictions. You might say the university was caught between a rock and a hard place—and it did indeed relax the rules.

Nationally, the tobacco industry contributes some $2.5 million a year to political campaigns—national, state, and sometimes even local races. Once, this money was focused on politicians from tobacco-growing states (with some exceptions) and was divided fairly equally between Republicans and Democrats. Between 1979 and 1982, for example, the top three recipients of tobacco monies in the U.S. Senate were Kentucky's Wendell H. Ford, a Democrat ($97,523); North Carolina's Terry Sanford, also a Democrat ($83,499); and North Carolina's Jesse Helms, a Republican ($82,000) well known for his leadership on conservative issues and for his opposition to civil rights, unions, women's rights, and gay and lesbian concerns.

More recently, however, tobacco companies have started giving money not just to individual campaigns, for which there are federal limits on how much any one group can give, but also to political parties, the so-called soft money donations, which are unlimited. In the first half of 1995, the top three contributors of soft money to the Republican Party were cigarette manufacturers, who gave a total of $1.3 million, almost 2/3 of which came from Philip Morris. At the same time, the Democrats received about $51,000 in soft money from the tobacco companies.

As you can see from these figures, the donations are no longer quite so evenly divided. On March 22, 1996, an episode of the PBS show *Washington Week in Review* focused on tobacco issues. Jeff Birnbaum of *Time* magazine described the new political climate:

> The tobacco industry is increasingly giving money hand over fist to Republicans, not to Democrats. The two top soft money givers, that is the big money givers, to the Republican Party are the two largest tobacco companies—somewhere in the range of $2 million, which is about six times the amount that they gave Democrats. This reverses a historic trend where the tobacco companies gave pretty evenly to the Democrats and Republicans. And I am told by tobacco people that that giving is actually accelerating and it's making a difference . . . And what they are getting for their choosing sides, though, they think, is worth the trade-off. The leaders—the Republican leaders in both the House and the Senate, have made clear to the rank and file that there will be no anti-tobacco legislation of any kind in this session, and that is exactly what has been happening.

In fact, as we saw, not only was there no antitobacco legislation in 1996, but the antitobacco bill of 1998 was defeated as well—primarily by Republicans.

Tobacco companies don't give money just to politicians. They also give it to cultural and educational groups. Philip Morris, in particular, has been an active supporter of a variety of arts projects, particularly in the African-American community. Groups such as Dance Theater of Harlem and the United Negro College Fund receive generous grants from tobacco companies.

Tobacco companies also spend money on advertising in various newspapers and magazines. How does this source of income affect the decisions of publishers to cover smoking and tobacco-related issues? No one can say for sure, but an article published in 1989 in the *New England Journal of Medicine* found that "coverage of smoking and health issues decreased by 65% in magazines that carried cigarette advertising, as compared with a decrease of 29% in magazines that did not."

Evaluating the Tobacco Industry

One of the goals of this book is to provide you with enough information to make up your own mind about whether you want to smoke or not. But you're not just an individual with a body that can be affected by smoking, you're also a citizen, living in a country where you have the chance to make your voice heard on political issues. So as you think about yourself and smoking, you might want to ask yourself some questions like these:

- What role do I think the tobacco company should play in the economy?
- If fewer people smoke, how might that affect the people who depend on smoking for their livelihood? What could or should be done to help those people?
- What role should the tobacco industry play in the political process?

- How does the tobacco industry affect my community? Does it give money to institutions or groups that I care about? What do I think those groups should do?
- What about foreign exports of tobacco? Is tobacco just another product, as some people argue, or is it immoral to sell a dangerous substance, as other people argue?
- How do I feel about tobacco advertising? Do I agree with the people who say that restrictions on any kind of advertising are a restriction on free speech? Or do I think that some kinds of speech should be restricted?

What other questions do you have about tobacco, smoking, and the tobacco industry? (If you'd like to do more reading, talk to various organizations, or do some research on the Internet, take a look at Chapter 7 for some helpful resources.)

None of these are simple questions, and they don't have simple answers. But they are questions about issues that deeply affect your health, your community, your country, and your world. The answers and the questions you have today can help you act to shape your world tomorrow.

3

Smoking, Your Body, and Your Mind

Angelica is so impressed with the difference that smoking has made in Lynette's life that she decides to try a cigarette herself. To her dismay, she has a very strong negative reaction: First she gets dizzy, then she throws up. "Did you feel that way?" she asks Lynette, who lit up her own cigarette while Angelica was trying to smoke.

"Oh, no," Lynette answers, taking a deep drag. "I liked smoking right away. Like I said, it really calms me down."

"Really?" says Angelica. "That sounds nice." She feels bad that she doesn't get to enjoy the pleasant, calm feeling that Lynette is talking about, and she's pretty embarrassed about reacting like such a baby. Lucky that Lynette is such a good friend, or she'd be *really* mortified.

"Yes," says Lynette thoughtfully, "but it doesn't *just* calm me down. It also kind of wakes me up. Especially first thing in the morning. It just really gets me going. And when I have to study, it helps me focus. It's like, I block out everything except the cigarette—even if my little brother is making lots of noise, or if my dad has the TV on. And then I block out everything except my studying. Honestly, I don't know how I'd get along without it."

At the end of his second day of trying to quit, Clarence has still only smoked one or two cigarettes less than he usually does. He is somewhat upset—not *very* upset, he tells himself, just a *little* upset—that he couldn't cut back when he said he was going to. Now he's starting to take it personally—him versus the cigarettes.

On the other hand, though, he's thinking that cutting back is going to be fairly uncomfortable, and he doesn't really want to go through a lot of hassle. Now that he's thinking about it, smoking is connected to pretty much everything he does these days. He uses smoking to help him wake up in the morning and to help him unwind before bed at night. When he's hungrily waiting for the lunch hour, smoking helps him feel less hungry. After he's eaten, smoking helps him digest his food. When he's nervous, smoking calms him down. When he has to focus on a task, smoking helps him concentrate. When he feels sad or upset about something, smoking soothes him. When he's angry at someone, smoking helps him to chill out. When he does something he likes, such as watching a basketball game on TV or taking a slow, pleasant walk through his favorite part of town, a cigarette makes the moment just that much nicer.

Clarence realizes that it's going to be almost impossible for him to cut back. Just about every part of his day includes a cigarette, and he can't bear the thought of giving that up.

Vanessa is getting more and more worried about her throat. She thinks about bringing up the subject with one or both of her parents, but the last time she did that, she didn't get very far. So she decides to watch the *way* they smoke, to notice everything she can about when, how, and why. Maybe if she learns more about what they're doing, she can figure out how to ask them to stop—or at least figure out how *she* can avoid more of their smoke.

The first thing that Vanessa notices about her dad is that he's a chain smoker. He starts smoking practically the moment he gets out of bed, and as far as Vanessa can figure, he doesn't stop until the moment his head hits the pillow. (Vanessa hopes that he doesn't actually smoke in bed, because she's heard about terrible fires that have been started that way, when people fall asleep with a cigarette burning and the mattress catches fire.) Her dad drives a delivery truck, so he can smoke pretty much all day at work. He doesn't actually smoke *while* he's eating, but between the soup and the main course, the main course and dessert, he usually has at least part of a cigarette, which means that a cigarette is burning all through dinner.

Vanessa thinks that her dad always seems preoccupied and grouchy, so it's hard to say *what* cigarettes are doing for him. She knows he worries a lot about money, and recently, a lot of men got laid off at his job, so she knows he's worried about that too. "Of course," she thinks, "if he's *this* worried about things when he *is* smoking, imagine what he'd be like if he tried to quit!" And it's true that, as grouchy as he gets, he never actually loses his temper, so maybe cigarettes are helping to keep him on an even keel.

Vanessa's mom has a completely different personality. She always seems to get a lot of fun out of life. But she's also always really busy. She works hard as a nurse at a local hospital, and she has a lot to do at home, taking care of Vanessa and her four brothers. Plus she gets involved with lots of groups at their church, helping to plan the Christmas pageant, organizing bake sales and bazaars, teaching Sunday school. Vanessa does notice that just about the only time her mom sits still and does nothing is when she's smoking a cigarette.

Thinking About Addiction

When you think about the word *addiction,* what comes to mind? If that word doesn't do anything for you, think about the slang term for it: *hooked.* Or consider a slightly more general term: *dependent.* For any or all of these terms, what comes to mind? What questions do you have? What kind of person do you imagine?

In our society, the idea of addiction has gotten a lot of attention in the past several years. You've probably seen at least one made-for-TV movie about someone with a drug addiction or a problem with drinking. You may know someone who takes part in one of the "Anonymous" 12-step programs to help with addictions to alcohol, cocaine, or narcotics. You may have heard "addictions" described on talk shows, where the definition is often broadened to include people who are "addicted" not just to physical substances—alcohol, cocaine—but also to certain types of behavior—gambling, compulsive sexual activity, even shopping.

If all of this discussion has left you confused about what *addiction* really means, take heart. You're not alone. There's enormous confusion about this topic in our society at the moment. That's partly because no one really knows exactly what an addiction is (though people who can't define addiction may believe they know one when they see one) and partly because there are several different ways that people use the term.

Addiction and Withdrawal

A key part of the idea of addiction is the notion of *withdrawal.* Withdrawal is what happens to people when they stop getting the substance they've been addicted to. Far example, the symptoms of heroin withdrawal include insomnia (not being able to sleep), weakness, vomiting, cramps, pains in the bones and muscles of the back, muscle spasms, alternating between being hot and cold, violent yawning, severe sneezing, and, occasionally, a collapse of the cardiovascular system (the heart and blood vessels).

Withdrawal also includes psychological symptoms. Sometimes it's hard to tell the difference, since intense feelings can also produce physical reactions and vice versa. For example, if a person wants heroin and cannot get it, he or she will feel depressed and upset, or possibly also nervous and frightened. You can argue that these reactions come as part of the physical loss of the drug. But you can also say that the person is understandably upset about all the pain he or she is in. Or you can say that the psychological symptoms come because the person can't imagine getting through life without the assistance of heroin.

It's the psychological aspects of withdrawal that make it so hard to know exactly what an addiction is. It's pretty clear when someone is addicted to heroin, or alcohol, because no matter how they feel about not taking the substance, they have dramatic physical symptoms as soon as they stop. But what about something that is not physical, like gambling? If people are used to gambling and try to stop, they won't have muscle spasms and vomiting, like a heroin addict. But, like the addict, they may feel depressed, anxious, angry, or frightened. Does that mean that the person isn't really addicted to gambling or that being addicted is mainly a psychological phenomenon?

You might also feel anxious or depressed if you're used to telling your troubles to a friend and your friend moves away. Does that mean you're addicted to your friend? Is being dependent on a drug like heroin the same as being dependent on a behavior like gambling? Is either or both the same as being dependent on a "good" thing, such as a beloved friend, a quiet time alone, or a particular piece of music?

It's questions like these that have made it so difficult to answer the question about whether smoking is addictive or not—and if we say that it is, to know what we mean by that. Even scientists disagree. Former surgeon general C. Everett Koop believes without a doubt that nicotine—and the cigarettes, chewing tobacco, and cigars that contain it—is addictive. In the 1988 surgeon general's report, Koop listed what he considered the major elements of drug addiction:

- the user's behavior is controlled by a physical substance that affects the brain
- the drug is used despite damage to the person taking it or to society
- drug-seeking behavior can become more important than other priorities
- taking the drug feels good enough that the person wants to keep taking it
- the longer you take the drug, the more of it you need to take
- trying to quit produces withdrawal symptoms
- people who quit often go back and start again

All of these elements, wrote Koop, characterize the way people who smoke or chew tobacco behave. He added, ". . . most smokers admit that they would like to quit but have not been able to do so. Smokers who have repeatedly failed in their attempts to quit probably realize that smoking is more than just a simple habit."

But Stephen M. Raffle disagrees. Raffle, a practicing psychiatrist and former assistant clinical professor of psychiatry at the University of California School of Medicine at San Francisco, who spent more than 20 years working with people addicted to heroin, alcohol, amphetamines (speed), barbiturates (downers), and cocaine, testified before Congress that nicotine is *not* addictive. In testimony before the Subcommittee on Health and Environment of the House of Representatives Committee on Energy and Commerce—hearings called to consider policy on tobacco—Raffle said that smokers are clearly capable of quitting whenever they want to. He said, "At this time [1994] more people in America have quit smoking than are currently smoking and 90% to 95% of those people quit without medical intervention," as opposed to those addicted to heroin, alcohol, or other drugs, who usually need some kind of medical help to quit.

After all, Raffle said, "the entire lives of [real] drug addicts are consumed with obtaining as much of their drug as possible and staying intoxicated." In his view, this is simply not true of smokers. Also, if "real" drug addicts want to quit, they face ravaging physical symptoms of withdrawal. They, according to Raffle, "must make enormous life changes in order to successfully abstain. Their behavior patterns must be drastically altered and their social structure revolutionized in order for them to successfully rehabilitate. Smokers . . . do not have the same burden in order to change their behavior."

Who is right—Koop or Raffle? Or are there still other ways of thinking about addiction, ways that might help us better understand smoking and chewing tobacco?

Models of Addiction

Science writer David Krogh spends most of his book *Smoking: The Artificial Passion* reviewing the scientific literature on addiction. (If you're interested in thinking more about this issue, go check out his book; it's clear, fascinating, and a lot of fun to read.) Krogh says that part of the reason it's so hard to define addiction comes from the fact that our thinking is dominated by two contradictory models of this term.

Model #1: "It's a Disease"

Alcoholics Anonymous, a self-help group founded for people who have trouble with drinking, talks about addiction as a disease. In this model, some people are born a certain way, with a certain type of body chemistry. If they, say, take a drink, they will sooner or later become powerless to control their drinking. The only solution is for them to avoid the substance they've become addicted to. Once they're in contact with it, they have no control over their responses any more than someone with, say, an allergy to cats can keep from coughing and sneezing when a cat is present. In this view, people who *aren't* alcoholics—who aren't born with this disease—*can* drink. The liquor itself isn't the problem, but rather the alcoholic's inborn disease. (Although this model was first developed by people who were concerned about problem drinking, it has been extended to include problematic ways of behaving, such as gambling, overspending, or getting into certain types of bad relationships.)

Model #2: "The Dangerous Substance"

A competing model for addiction focuses on the power of a particular substance—say, heroin. In this model, the substance has all the power. Heroin, for example, is seen as such a potent substance that pretty much anybody who takes it a few times is going to feel that he or she can't live without it. Crack is also seen in this way, as a "highly addictive" substance that can pretty much turn anybody foolish enough to take it into an instant addict.

The Spectrum of Addiction

Krogh proposes a third way of thinking about addiction. He asks us to think of all addictions as somehow under our control and not as diseases that make us helpless. Whether we're talking about problem drinking, compulsive gambling, or a self-destructive pattern of relationships, Krogh suggests that there are choices that we can make, ways of getting help, and strategies for overcoming the addiction.

In this context, he proposes, we make room for elements of both the "disease" model and the "dangerous substance" model. Different people have different reactions to chemical substances, and genetics, body chemistry, psychology, and life circumstances probably all play some kind of role in how susceptible a given person is to a given substance.

However, some substances *are* problematic for the vast majority of people; we know this because these substances have generated widespread addictions in almost every society that has known them. With smoking, Krogh says, "the *use* of tobacco . . . is very nearly the same thing as the *addiction* that takes place: 90 percent of all smokers, at a minimum, cannot decide to use tobacco one day and then leave it alone the next."

Certainly, Krogh notes, the physical effects of quitting smoking are less intense than those of quitting heroin, and it's true that medical intervention is usually not required to deal with the symptoms (though some people may need other kinds of help in quitting). Still, he points out,

> three quarters of all smokers say they would like to stop. . . . What's keeping them from following through? As a clue, people who have tried to quit have given us plenty of descriptions like this [from an interview by Krogh with Josselyn, a middle-aged woman, in Berkeley, California]: "I'm telling you I wanted a cigarette so bad I cried. I did. And not just once but several times. I was so nervous I could hardly carry on at work, and I couldn't hide it. After awhile I would just shake. People said they couldn't see it, but I could feel it."

Krogh offers some other quotes that suggest the addictive power of nicotine. One is from Robert Hughes, describing life among prisoners in the penal colony of Australia early in the 1800s:

> A group of prisoners were being led in single file through the forest when, without provocation or warning, one of them crushed the skull of the prisoner in front of him with his ax. Later he explained that there was no tobacco to be had in the settlement; that he had been a smoker all his life and would rather die than go without it; so, in the torment of nicotine withdrawal, he had killed the man in order to be hanged himself.

And here's a letter from N. A. Photiades to the *Times* in London, written in 1957 about his memories of tobacco shortages during World War II:

> I had the misfortune to be a prisoner for nearly four years during the war and found that the one thing that men were unable to give up was cigarette smoking. There was, in fact,

a very active market in bartering the handful of rice we received daily for the two cigarettes our hosts so kindly gave us. I have actually seen men die of starvation because they had sold their food for cigarettes.

Finally, Krogh describes a study conducted in the 1980s by Lynn Kozlowski and others at the Addiction Research Center Foundation in Toronto. The researchers asked some of their patients, "Think of your strongest urge to use cigarettes, and then think of your strongest urge to use alcohol or the drug that brought you here for treatment. Which was stronger?" Some two-thirds of the patients said that their urges for cigarettes were as strong or stronger than their urges for alcohol, while some 20 percent said that their urges for cigarettes was as strong as or stronger than their urge for heroin.

The "Nervous-System" Drug

We still haven't explained just what it is about nicotine that makes it such an attractive drug. To begin to answer this question, we have to look at the body's chemistry.

Say, as you read this book, you'd like to turn the page. Have you ever wondered how the thought gets translated from your brain to your hand? The answer is through our *nervous system,* the pathways of nerves that transmit information from the brain throughout the body (for action) and from the body to the brain (to report sensations of hot, cold, pain, pleasure, and so on). The nerves in our brain and nervous system don't exactly hook up. Instead, there are tiny gaps, called synapses, between nerves. For messages to be sent—for us to move and take action, or to experience physical sensations—something has to jump that gap.

Enter the neurotransmitters, chemicals that jump the gaps in our bodies and brains, allowing us to act and feel. To send even a single, simple message through our body

("Turn that page!"), neurotransmitters must jump hundreds of thousands of gaps.

Think of a neurotransmitter as a person swinging from one trapeze to another. Without the second trapeze, however, the neurotransmitter can't jump. In your body and brain, that second trapeze is another chemical, a receptor designed to pick up and receive the neurotransmitter. We've got dozens of neurotransmitters flowing through our system. And not every receptor picks up every neurotransmitter. Each receptor is specialized and will receive only the neurotransmitter for which it has been designed, so a receptor needs to be where it's supposed to be for messages to flow smoothly.

Now, imagine if there were a chemical that mimicked one of our key neurotransmitters, such as the neurotransmitter acetylcholine, or ACH for short. ACH operates everywhere that nerves and muscles meet. It's the chemical that must be present for the muscles in your hand to hear the page-turning message sent by your brain. Early in the 20th century, scientists discovered that nicotine mimics this important body chemical—to such an extent that the receptors that pick up ACH are known as nicotinic receptors.

If all nicotine did was mimic ACH, that alone would make it a very powerful drug for the human body. But nicotine also stimulates other bodily functions. For example, the adrenal glands have the job of releasing norepinephrine and epinephrine, hormones better known as adrenaline. Whenever you're under some extra stress—there's a test to take, an enemy to outwit, a potential boyfriend or girlfriend to woo—your adrenal glands release some extra adrenaline. This chemical gets your heart pumping extra blood so that your muscles can operate at peak efficiency. (This is a holdover from the days when extra stresses meant physical danger—a bear to outrun, a mammoth to slay—and required a person to either "fight" or take "flight.") Nicotine in the human body stimulates the adrenal glands, gets the heart pumping extra hard, and raises the blood pressure. (Blood pressure is a measurement of how the blood is circulating in the body. If the heart is pumping extra hard and blood is circulating extra fast, blood pressure goes up.) That's why smokers get such a lift from that first cigarette of the day: It sets their hearts pumping at an extra 10 to 20 beats per minute and raises their blood pressure by 5 to 10 points.

Now you know why Lynette said that nicotine wakes her up and gets her going. She's not just talking about a feeling; her heart is actually beating faster, and her blood is rushing through her veins. From her body's point of view, she's getting ready to face a serious challenge, and all her resources are being pulled together to meet it.

This may feel good sometimes. Lynette certainly likes it, and so do the millions of coffee drinkers, who get a similar rush from their caffeine. The problem is that the body isn't designed for that type of reaction without the physical activity to back it up. When you get an adrenaline rush—whether it's from nervousness, excitement, smoking, caffeine, or some other drug—your body really does crave "fight or flight." Your blood is pumping so that you'll run, or fight, or lift a heavy weight, or climb a steep mountain—anything to use up that excess energy you've just generated. People who don't work off that energy physically or diffuse it gently by relaxing and finding other ways to combat stress are putting their heart under some serious strain. This is one of the reasons that smoking and heart disease go together.

One of the best actors I ever worked with—a lifetime smoker—had major heart trouble by the time he was in his early 40s and had to undergo open-heart surgery. He quit for a while, but less than a year later, he started again. I'll never forget the shock of the call from his girlfriend, informing me that three days ago, my friend and colleague had collapsed on the street from a heart attack. Because he didn't have any identification on him, he was simply taken to the hospital, where he died, alone. None of us knew what had happened or where he was until his body was finally identified a few days later. He wasn't even 45 years old.

But I'm veering away from the subject at hand. Let's go back to the neurotransmitters for a minute. We've seen why nicotine stimulates people. But Lynette—and Vanessa's mother, and other smokers—also find it relaxing. Why is that?

The Drug That Stuns Elephants

Remember in Chapter 1 when we learned that nicotine in sufficient quantities could tranquilize a large elephant? A miniature version of that reaction is felt by smokers every day. For an explanation, we have to look once again at the way the brain and nervous system work.

Let's revisit that neurotransmitter, jumping from one nerve to the next like a trapeze artist flying over the gap between two trapezes. Remember that the second trapeze—technically known as a receptor site—must receive the jumpy neurotransmitter. If there isn't enough of the receptor chemical at the site, or if something else goes wrong, the message won't get through.

So in *small* doses, nicotine helps this process along. As we saw, it mimics ACH and swings merrily through the body, sending the heart muscle a "speed-up" message and sending the adrenal glands the "release adrenaline" message.

But in *large* doses, guess what happens? The nicotine shoves the ACH out of the way and takes up all the room on the receptors, like a big, jealous trapeze artist who got there first and wants to steal the limelight from all the other performers. So if a person is feeling stressed, and there's enough nicotine in his or her system, the stress messages can't get through. There just isn't a free receptor to pick them up. (In fact, an overdose of nicotine—taken, say, by injection—could kill you: The message to your lungs to breathe would never get through because nicotine is blocking the circuits.)

The "High-Performance" Drug

What about Lynette's claim that nicotine helps her concentrate? And how about the way that Vanessa's father seems to be slightly less angry when he smokes?

It's hard to be completely definite and the evidence is contradictory, but many studies suggest that nicotine *might* have the following effects:

- reducing aggression
- improving concentration in the face of noise and other distraction
- helping with repetitive tasks that require long-lasting concentration
- reducing boredom
- keeping people on an even keel, especially in the face of stress or boredom

Wow! A drug that can actually help people perform better, especially at jobs that are repetitive, boring, stressful, or otherwise frustrating. A drug that can make people less angry and aggressive in situations where bosses, teachers, family members, and others might be getting on their nerves. A drug that allows people to "chill out" while staying wide awake and working well. Sounds like a miracle drug, doesn't it?

There are only two problems.

1) To get the pleasures of nicotine, instead of the agonies of withdrawal, you need to maintain a fairly constant level of the drug in your body. That's why 90 percent of the people who smoke can't just "take it or leave it alone." Even problem drinkers might only binge on weekends. "Problem smokers," which is just about everybody who smokes, have to stay "high" all the time. The only time that nicotine levels in their bodies fall is at night, when they're asleep, which is why most smokers wake up just dying for a cigarette.

2) This miracle drug is likely to kill you. It's not just that it takes, on average, eight years off your life. It's also that the *ways* that nicotine kills—heart disease, emphysema, lung cancer and other lung diseases, other cancers—are particularly agonizing. The smoker is usually in for years of misery before death finally comes.

OK, that's the grim outlook regarding the heart, circulatory, and nervous systems. Let's move on and find out why nicotine is so bad for the lungs.

Breathe Deeply

Seriously. Take a deep breath. Pull the air all the way down into your stomach (technically, your diaphragm), and let the breath out slowly.

What you just did—that single breath—made use of one of the body's most amazing organs, the lung. The lungs' best-known function, of course, is to draw oxygen into our bodies, the oxygen that we require to live. A shortage of oxygen quickly affects our brain, our heart, our liver, our kidneys, and every other organ in our body.

The lungs also expel carbon dioxide, the gas that is left over after metabolism, the process of breaking food down and converting it into the energy that we need to live. When the lungs can't exhale enough carbon dioxide, the gas stays in the body—and poisons it. In extreme cases, such as when a person and a car are enclosed together in a small space, the car's exhaust, which is loaded with carbon monoxide, can be fatal. In less extreme cases, such as those of cigarette smokers, the excess carbon monoxide may not kill instantly, but it does damage the brain, heart, and other organs.

The lungs are also an extremely large organ. The total surface area of both lungs is more than 100 square yards—that's about as big as a tennis court. Yet the membrane that transmits oxygen to the blood and receives carbon monoxide from the blood is only $1/50$ the thickness of a piece of tissue paper.

Ideally, of course, we should all go through life with two perfectly healthy, functioning lungs. But here's a fascinating fact: An otherwise healthy person who has had one entire lung and a third of the remaining lung removed can still breathe comfortably. So when smokers have "shortness of breath," that means they've already lost two-thirds of their total lung capacity.

What Happens When You Smoke

How does the smoke from cigarettes affect the lungs? The nicotine enters the body in little droplets. Each tiny drop of nicotine is suspended—carried—in a solid particle of partly burned tobacco, known as *tar*. So-called low-tar cigarettes are made in such a way that they produce fewer particles of tobacco.

Why is tar a concern? Because those little particles are so small, they can make their way into the farthest reaches of the lungs. The lungs are cleverly constructed: The part that connects to your nose and throat, where you breathe in air from the outside, is fairly large, like the trunk of a tree. But this large "trunk" breaks into smaller and smaller "branches," and then into tiny "twigs" called alveoli. The place where oxygen crosses over from the lung into the blood is at the smallest, most delicate portion of the lungs. And those delicate places are where the droplets of nicotine, each in its little particle of tar, cross over into the bloodstream.

Just how serious is this assault on the smoker's lungs? According to tests done by R.J. Reynolds, the tobacco smoke particles inhaled by a smoker are 10,000 times more concentrated than automobile pollution at rush hour on a freeway.

It's because cigarette smoke is inhaled that smokers get such a fast hit. Swallowing a drug means that the substance must go into the stomach, where it takes about half an hour to cross into the bloodstream. Injecting a substance into the blood with a hypodermic needle is a lot faster than that. But breathing nicotine is also pretty fast. It only takes about eight seconds for the first puff of a cigarette to be felt in the heart, lungs, and brain.

So when that first drag goes deep into the lungs, it passes almost instantly into the bloodstream, and here's what happens next.

- The heart speeds up, from 10 to 20 beats per minute.
- The blood vessels constrict, or tighten, so that blood pressure goes up 5 to 10 points.
- The temperature of the skin drops by 6 degrees Fahrenheit (that's because the blood is rushing to the heart, where it would be needed in a real crisis—the "fight or flight" reaction we talked about).
- The level of blood sugar—the body's store of energy—falls, again because the blood sugar is being burned up in this stressed-out reaction.
- The hypothalamus, which regulates hunger, gets one of those "speed-up" messages, so the appetite falls, too. (We'll look more at the relationship between nicotine, appetite, and weight loss in Chapter 4.)

Low Tar and High Ammonia

Before we move on to the actual effects of nicotine on the lungs, let's look a little more closely at just what's in that cigarette. One of the biggest controversies surrounding the "secret documents" of the tobacco companies was the evidence of all the various additives that cigarette companies put in their cigarettes to increase the potency of nicotine. For example, the FDA found that Brown & Williamson (owned by the British American Tobacco Company) added some 599 chemicals to cigarettes.

One of these ingredients is ammonia. As John Fahs says in his book *Cigarette Confidential,* adding ammonia to cigarettes makes the nicotine in tobacco more accessible to smokers and thereby makes the cigarette more addictive. Fahs explains, "Only a fraction of the nicotine in cigarette tobacco gets inhaled by the smoker; ammonia technology thus allows more of the drug to be delivered to the user." It also means that cigarette smokers' lungs are being daily exposed to ammonia and a host of other chemicals as well as the tar and nicotine we already knew about.

But, you may be wondering, what about so-called low-tar cigarettes? Aren't they easier on the lungs than the regular kind?

It's true that low-tar cigarettes do introduce fewer particles of tar into the lung. However, the tar that enters a smoker's body even from "low-tar" cigarettes is still a fairly large amount. It's still enough to place considerable stress on the lungs—and it's still a *carcinogen,* or cancer-causing agent.

Also, low-tar cigarettes taste different and deliver less nicotine, so most smokers will inhale low-tar cigarettes longer and more deeply to get the same nicotine hit that they're used to from regular cigarettes. In fact, the secret documents seemed to show that tobacco companies added various ingredients to the low-tar product, both to mimic the flavor of regular cigarettes and to increase their nicotine output. You might say low-tar cigarettes are a case of taking away with one hand and putting back with the other.

Assault on the Lungs

So picture the average smoker breathing in tobacco smoke a couple hundred times a day. Each drag floods his or her lungs with tar, ammonia, and a host of other ingredients. How do the lungs react?

Here's a list of the various types of lung diseases believed to be caused by smoking. These diseases all have other causes as well, including air pollution and exposure to cancer-causing agents at work. But smoking is the leading cause of preventable disease, disability, and death in the United States, in large part because of its tendency to cause the following conditions:

- *Lung cancer.* Cancer is characterized by the uncontrolled growth of abnormal cells. These abnormal cells form lumps, or tumors, that invade normal tissues and keep body parts from doing their job. Sometimes tumors form that are *not* cancerous, that is, they will not spread to other parts of the body. These tumors are called *benign.* Other tumors, however, are cancerous. They have the potential to spread from a single place throughout the entire body, eventually resulting in death. These tumors are called *malignant.*

  Lung cancer is the uncontrolled growth of these abnormal cells in the lungs. Some 15 percent of all cancer cases in the United States are lung cancer, and there were 178,000 new cases in 1997. More than 1/4 (28 percent) of cancer deaths in the United States are deaths from lung cancer. The number-one cause of lung cancer is tobacco smoke.

  Remember how we said that not *all* of the diseases on this list were caused by smoking? Well, that's true, but 85 percent of all people who are diagnosed with lung cancer are current or former smokers.

  Symptoms of lung cancer include a nagging cough; chest, shoulder, or back pain that feels like a constant ache; shortness of breath; fatigue; weight loss; repeated bouts of pneumonia or bronchitis; coughing up blood; hoarseness; unexplained weakness in the legs; and swelling of the neck and face. Lung cancer spreads rapidly to other parts of the body, which can cause pain, headaches, bleeding, weakness, bone fractures, or blood clots.

It's hard to treat lung cancer; there isn't really any cure. One approach is to have surgery to cut out all or part of a lung. If the cancer has spread to another lung or another part of the body, or if the person is not in good shape, then treatments include radiation therapy in which the tumors are exposed to radiation to try to reduce or eliminate them; and chemotherapy in which the patient is given drugs to try to kill the cancer cells. Since both the radiation and the chemicals have the goal of killing cells, they naturally place a strain on the patient's entire body. People are often very sick during this treatment. In radiation therapy, it's common for people to lose their hair. Other side effects of both treatments include nausea and weakness.

- **Emphysema.** This lung disease is *chronic,* which means that once you have it, it doesn't go away, although sometimes it's more severe than others. Its main symptom is shortness of breath. It's caused by lungs losing their elasticity—the way a stretched-out rubber band does—so that parts of the lung becomes enlarged. The enlarged areas trap stale air, making it difficult for the lungs to expel the old air and breathe in the new. As a result, the blood doesn't get enough oxygen, and patients might end up with too much carbon dioxide in their systems. As we saw, that can be a problem for the brain, heart, and other organs.

  Although the causes of emphysema aren't fully understood, smoking is generally considered to be the most important cause.

- **Chronic bronchitis.** Again, *chronic* bronchitis is a version of the disease that patients have more or less

permanently. Sometimes they're in better shape, sometimes they're suffering, but the bronchitis never really
goes away. It's caused by the breathing tubes, or *bronchi,*
being inflamed, or irritated. As air rubs up and down
these irritated passageways, the body produces mucus,
which blocks the airways and makes the patient feel as
though he or she is choking. As a result, the patient
coughs, trying to get the mucus out. Chronic bronchitis
(as opposed to a one-time hit of the disease) lasts at least
three months out of a year, two years in a row.

Again, the causes of chronic bronchitis aren't fully
understood. But smoking is generally considered to be
its most important cause.

• ***Asthma.*** Asthma is a rather mysterious disease. For
unexplained reasons the number of asthma cases has
been growing by leaps and bounds in the last two or
three decades. Some types of asthma seemed to be
caused by factors in a person's body that nobody really
understands. Other types seemed to be triggered by
outside causes, such as air pollution, pollen, cold air, and
cigarette smoke. Although scientists are still figuring this
all out, it seems as though exposure to cigarette
smoke—whether from the cigarettes you smoke yourself
or from the smoking of those around you—can trigger
an asthma attack. Sometimes cigarette smoke will trigger
an attack in someone who has never shown any signs of
asthma before.

Cigars

Since 1993, sales of big cigars and little cigarillos have been
on the rise—up 45 percent for a total of 4.4 billion cigars
sold in 1996, the highest level since the mid-1980s. The use
of premium cigars—the really expensive kind that cost
more than $10 apiece—has risen 250 percent since 1993.

Teenage cigar use is up as well. According to "1998 Facts and Figures" from the American Cancer Society, in 1996, some 6 million people aged 14 to 19 (26.7 percent of the people in this age group) said they'd smoked a cigar in the past year.

Cigars have gotten lots of good press in the 1990s. Many celebrities started smoking cigars in the 1990s, and the bad press of the cigarette companies have the dubious effect of making cigar companies look good by comparison. Nonetheless, the 1989 U.S. surgeon general's report had plenty to say about the health hazards of cigars.

- Most of the same cancer-causing chemicals that are found in cigarettes are present in cigars too.
- Deaths from all types of cancer among men who smoke cigars are 34 percent higher than among nonsmokers.
- Generally, users of tobacco of all types—cigarettes, cigars, pipes, and smokeless tobacco—are 5 to 10 times more likely to get mouth or throat cancer than nonsmokers are.
- Cigar smokers are particularly at risk of cancer of the mouth, esophagus, or larynx (voice box); they are 4 to 10 times more likely than nonsmokers to get one of those types of cancer.

According to the Coalition for Accountability, cigar smokers are also up to 3.6 times more likely than nonsmokers to die from chronic obstructive pulmonary disease, a disease, such as emphysema or chronic bronchitis, that interferes with the workings of the lungs.

Smokeless Tobacco

Smokeless tobacco—chewing tobacco and snuff—has been growing in popularity among teenage boys. According to the Centers for Disease Control and Prevention's Youth Risk

Behavior Survey, some 20 percent of male high school students used smokeless tobacco in 1995. That's a huge percentage, when you consider that in 1992–1993 (the last year for which figures are available on adults), only 4.0 percent of men and 0.4 percent of women used smokeless tobacco. And in 1994, only 7 percent of men aged 18 to 24 years reported the use of smokeless tobacco.

Here's another indicator of the increased use of smokeless tobacco. According to the U.S. Department of Agriculture, U.S. output of moist snuff has risen 83 percent, from about 30 million pounds in 1981 to some 57 million pounds in 1996.

There are various ways to use smokeless tobacco; "dipping snuff" is the one that has health professionals most concerned. Tobacco in this form is pressed into a coarse, moist powder. The user puts it between his or her cheek and gum, and from it the nicotine is absorbed through the tissue in the mouth.

As with cigarettes, the effects of nicotine in smokeless tobacco—stimulating and relaxing, possibly aiding concentration and reducing aggression—are felt by the user. Also as with cigarettes, the user almost certainly wants to keep a constant level of nicotine in his or her system—for example, by dipping snuff regularly throughout the day—to avoid the effects of withdrawal. In this case, too, the user is subject to all the cancer-causing agents that come out of the tobacco and cross into the body along with the nicotine.

The U.S. surgeon general studied smokeless tobacco in 1986 and concluded that this was "not a safe substitute for smoking cigarettes. It can cause cancer and a number of noncancerous oral conditions and can lead to nicotine addiction and dependence." In fact, mouth cancer is much more frequent among people who dip snuff than among people who don't put nicotine into their mouths, and the risk of cancer of the cheek and gum is nearly 50 times higher for smokeless tobacco than for nonusers. In addition, the nicotine in smokeless tobacco places the same kind of strain on the heart and blood pressure as does nicotine in any other form.

Smokeless tobacco is also bad for the mouth in other ways. It causes gums to pull back from the teeth, which both looks awful and means the person could lose a tooth. It leads to other kinds of gum disease, as well. People who chew smokeless tobacco or who dip snuff are prone to cavities and discolored teeth. And, as you might expect, it causes *halitosis,* or bad breath.

Something in the Air . . .

One of the hottest smoking-related debates in recent years has been the controversy over *secondhand smoke,* also known as *environmental tobacco smoke* (ETS). A wide range of public health groups claim that secondhand smoke—the smoke from a person's cigarette that is inhaled by people nearby—is almost as bad for you as the smoke that a person inhales from his or her own cigarette.

"Cigarettes don't just kill people who smoke," says Carol M. Browner, administrator at the Environmental Protection Agency (EPA). "They also kill people who choose not to smoke. We have a responsibility to protect children and adults from involuntary exposure to other peoples' smoke."

In her 1994 Congressional testimony, Browner put forward the EPA's recommendations:

- People shouldn't smoke in their own homes or let others do so.
- Places where children spend time—schools, day care centers, and the like—should protect children from secondhand smoke.
- People at work should be able to spend the entire day in smoke-free areas.
- Smoking sections in restaurants or bars should be set up in such a way as to keep nonsmokers from having to be exposed to secondhand smoke.

The result of the EPA's position—which drew on the positions taken by other groups during the 1980s—was a new widespread concern with the dangers of secondhand smoke. Many cities and states began to require no-smoking sections in restaurants; some places, like New York City, outlawed smoking in many kinds of restaurants. Lots of offices and other workplaces became no-smoking zones; so did national and some international flights. People who supported these measures were likely to cite the long list of dangers that the EPA linked to secondhand smoke in a 1993 report:

- Some 3,000 nonsmoking adults die of diseases caused by exposure to secondhand smoke every year.
- Secondhand smoke causes coughing, phlegm, chest discomfort, and reduced lung function in nonsmokers.
- U.S. infants and children under 18 months of age suffer some 150,000 to 300,000 respiratory tract infections (lung diseases such as pneumonia and bronchitis) every year, leading to 7,500–15,000 hospitalizations.
- Children exposed to secondhand smoke at home are more likely to have middle-ear disease and reduced lung function.
- Some 2 to 5 million U.S. children suffer from asthma; of these, about 20 percent experience more asthma attacks—and more severe attacks—than their fellow young asthmatics, due to secondhand smoke.
- Secondhand smoke contains more than 4,000 chemical compounds, including carbon monoxide (which poisons the human body), ammonia, formaldehyde, and other poisons. Four of the chemicals—benzene, 2-naphthylamine, 4-aminobiphenyl, and polonium-210—are classified by the EPA as known carcinogens—cancer-causing agents. Ten other chemicals are classified as probable carcinogens. Regarding environmental tobacco smoke, the American Lung Association has summed up its dangers in the following numbers: Of the more than 4,000

chemicals in environmental tobacco smoke, 200 are poisons and 43 cause cancer. In fact, environmental tobacco smoke itself has been classified as a class-A carcinogen—a known, dangerous, cancer-causing agent—by the EPA, in the same category as such substances as asbestos.

Other public health groups have claimed that ETS is linked to several types of cancers, lung disease, heart problems, stroke, and hardening of the arteries, as well as to problems in pregnancy, miscarriage, low birthweight, and Sudden Infant Death Syndrome (SIDS).

The EPA's position on secondhand smoke was not without its opponents. Matthew Hoffman, an adjunct policy analyst at the conservative Competitive Enterprise Institute, spoke for many critics when he wrote that the EPA's 1993 report was simply bad science. In a 1993 article in the conservative magazine *Human Events,* Hoffman did a statistical analysis of the EPA's report in which he argued that the government agency had failed to find a convincing link between secondhand smoke and cancer.

"The EPA's disregard for scientific standards threatens to open up American homes and offices to costly and intrusive regulations, and creates a precedent that might be used to indict other aspects of our living environment," Hoffman warned. "Unfortunately, few voices have risen to challenge the EPA's flaunting of scientific standards. The tobacco industry's Tobacco Institute has been one of the few dissenting voices in the debate, and for obvious reasons it has been ignored as a tool of financial interests."

"However," Hoffman continued, "the EPA should not be treated as an impartial source of scientific truth, because it has similar incentives to argue that ETS is a carcinogen. With every substance EPA classifies as cancer-causing, the agency increases its budget, gains power and prestige, and opens new vistas for its regulatory activities."

Hoffman's position was echoed on July 19, 1998, when a federal judge found that the EPA had made procedural and scientific mistakes in its 1993 report. "Any legislative body that was considering passing a law based on the E.P.A. report is going to have to rethink it," said Seth Moskowitz, a spokesperson for the R.J. Reynolds Tobacco Company.

Judge William L. Osteen Sr. of the federal district court in Greensboro, North Carolina—a major tobacco-growing state—criticized the report partly because it was written by a panel that did not include any representatives of the tobacco industry. "In this case, E.P.A. publicly committed to a conclusion before research had begun," Judge Osteen wrote.

The EPA, however, stood by its report—and by the antismoking ordinances that the report had inspired over the years. "Inasmuch as the tobacco guys will claim that secondhand smoke has no health effects, we are clearly upset," said EPA administrator Browner. "But the important thing that people should understand is that secondhand smoke is a real health risk. Nothing in this ruling should be used to overturn any public health decision taken by any business or any city to ban smoking."

For anyone who isn't used to analyzing statistics, the argument over the EPA report may be hard to follow. In this case, you might want to draw your conclusions based on the two sides of the debate. Those who say that secondhand smoke is a danger include many major public health organizations, both public and private, including the surgeon general's office, the National Academy of Sciences, the National Institute of Occupational Safety and Health, the National Cancer Institute, the American Cancer Society, the Emphysema Foundation, and the American Lung Association. Those who say that the danger has been exaggerated include the tobacco industry's Tobacco Institute and a number of conservative policy institutes, including Hoffman's Competitive Enterprise Institute.

Thinking About Smoking

Now you've got the basic information about what smoking does to your body, and you've heard both sides of the debates about nicotine addiction and secondhand smoke. If collecting facts were all you needed to make a decision, you'd be all set.

But, as Angelica, Clarence, and Vanessa have found, just knowing a group of facts isn't always enough. Sometimes you have to figure out how to weigh and evaluate the facts in order to come up with the decision that's right for you. In the next three chapters, we'll talk about different ways of making choices—about smoking, about quitting, and about taking action on this very important issue.

4

Making Decisions About Smoking

Angelica decides to give cigarettes another try. She finds that after a couple of weeks of smoking a cigarette now and then, they don't make her sick any more. If she wanted to, she really could start smoking regularly—just the way Lynette does.

So now Angelica has a decision to make: does she want to start smoking regularly? On the one hand, she still thinks that Lynette looks very cool when she smokes. Lynette now hangs out with a group of other kids at school who smoke, and, as long as Angelica doesn't smoke, she feels left out. Worse, she feels that these other kids are laughing at her for being a baby. Plus, she'd like to get the same lift that Lynette seems to get from smoking, and it also sounds nice to have a way to keep calm.

On the other hand, Angelica has noticed that Lynette seems to be smoking more and more often. Lynette may not mind, but Angelica doesn't like the idea of being out of control, *dependent* on something outside herself. Also, smoking more means that Lynette has less to spend on pizza and after-school snacks, because she's got to make sure she can afford three or four packs of cigarettes each week.

Angelica knows about the health risks of smoking, but it's hard to believe they apply to her. After all, she's *not* an athlete or a singer, so she reasons that there's no immediate concern. The other health problems—lung cancer, emphysema, heart disease—seem *very* far in the future. "If I think I'm going to get sick, I could just quit smoking," Angelica thinks to herself.

As she goes back and forth between the pros and cons, Angelica feels more confused than ever. What should she do?

Clarence feels caught in a double bind. On the one hand, realizing how hard it is for him to quit makes him want to just keep smoking. Why should he give up a habit that he enjoys, especially when it's going to be so difficult and unpleasant to stop? On the other hand, the whole idea that smoking isn't within his control makes Clarence mad. Part of him wants to quit just to prove that he can.

Also, Clarence sometimes feels as though it's him versus the cigarette companies. He knows that they're targeting young African-American men as future smokers, and it makes him mad to think he's just another statistic to them. It gives him the feeling that they've won and he's lost.

Clarence still isn't sure he wants to quit, though. He keeps going back and forth, thinking about how hard quitting will be and how much he likes that first cigarette of the day, how nice it is to relax with a smoke. Then he sees another newspaper story about tobacco companies advertising in the inner cities or about lung cancer rates going up among African Americans, and he feels like quitting all over again.

He really isn't sure how to make this decision.

Vanessa decides that it's not realistic to ask her parents to quit smoking. After all, smoking is their decision, just like not smoking is her decision. What she *can* do, she decides, is try to work out a compromise that might protect her from the worst effects of their smoke.

Vanessa sits down at her desk, turns a piece of paper sideways, and draws a line across it. At the left-hand end of the line, she makes a list called "What It's Like Now." That list includes such things as "Mom & Dad smoking all the time," "throat getting sore," "trouble singing," "smoke at mealtimes," "every room except mine filled with smoke." Vanessa doesn't worry about spelling, grammar, or logic. She just puts down everything she can think of in no particular order.

At the right-hand end of the line, she makes another list called "What I'd Like." There the list includes items such as "No smoke anywhere in the house," "throat healed," "good singing," "parents healthy and live long."

In the center of the line, Vanessa tries to think of changes she could request that would be between the way things are and the way she'd ideally like them to be. She tries to think about compromises that her parents might make and that she might be able to live with. Although she isn't nearly as sure about this list, she tries writing down a few items, just to see what they look like: "no smoke at mealtimes," "smoke only in parents' bedroom," "if they can't quit, cut down," "switch to low-tar cigarettes," "smoke only outside the house."

Vanessa isn't sure yet what she wants to say to her parents, but making a list helps her focus her thoughts.

How Do You Make Decisions?

When was the last time you made an important decision? You might have been deciding about what classes to take, whether to continue with music lessons, how to handle a difficult problem with family or friends, or some other choice that affected your life.

Here's an exercise that can help you learn a lot about yourself. Choose some decision that feels important to you, and ask yourself the following questions about how you made it. There are no right or wrong answers—but the answers you find may tell you something about who you are.

- **What factors did I consider in my choice?** These might include "how my family would feel," "what my friends were doing," "my health," "my personal likes and dislikes," "my fear of bad consequences such as [you fill in the blank]," "my hope that [again, fill the blank]," "what people would think of me," "how I feel about myself," "what I think is right and wrong," and many other factors. Take a minute to jot down any factor that you ever thought about as you wrestled with your decision.
- **What factors were most important?** Think about what you finally decided. Then underline, circle, or highlight two or three items on your list that ended up being most important in making your choice.
- **What do these factors say about me as a person?** How we make choices is one of the most important things about us. The teenage years are especially exciting—and difficult—because we're finally old enough to make choices about things that our parents or other outside factors once decided for us. Starting in adolescence and continuing for the rest of our life, the choices we make tell ourselves and the world what kind of people we are. Take a few minutes to write down whatever answers come to mind as you ask yourself what your decision-making process says about you. You might jot down some unconnected notes or write out your feelings in complete sentences. Make it a long answer or a short one; either way, it's your chance to discover something new about yourself.
- **How do I feel about this choice now?** Are you happy with the decision you made? Why or why not? Again,

take a few minutes to write how you feel, either in brief notes or in full sentences. Keep in mind that we often have mixed feelings about even the best decisions, so be as specific as you can. Are there some parts of the decision that you like and others that you don't? Are you happy with your part in the decision but not so happy about how other people reacted? Write down everything you can about what you did, what happened, and how you felt about it.

- **What have I learned by doing this exercise?** Finally, write freely, in any form that works for you, about how you feel right now. Are you happy, unhappy, or both with what you've learned about yourself? Does anything ·about the process—either what you did before or thinking about it now—make you sad? Angry? Happy? Ashamed? Proud? Would you decide in a different way the next time, or do you feel renewed confidence in your decision-making process? Remember, nobody but you will ever see these notes, so be as honest and complete as you can.

Making decisions, living with the consequences, and deciding whether or not we want to make new decisions is one of the hardest—and most satisfying—parts of growing up. When you're a child, it sometimes seems as though adults have all the power and all the fun. After all, they get to decide whatever they want, and you, the child, have to live with their decision.

As you become first a teenager and then an adult, you start to realize that it's not so simple. Yes, you have more choices to make, but then you have to live with the consequences of your choices. These consequences can include

- **physical effects**—how good your health is, how much money you have to spend, what kind of clothes you have to wear

- *emotional effects*—how you feel about yourself, your decision, and your life in general
- *social effects*—how you treat other people, including your friends and family; how other people treat you; what options are now open or closed to you

As you read the rest of this chapter, and as you think about smoking in general, keep in mind that to smoke or not to smoke is finally *your* decision. You're the one who has to make that decision—every day of your life. You're also the one who has to live with the consequences. Weighing the consequences and choosing wisely is one of the most important decisions you'll ever have to make.

Why Do People Smoke?

Most major life decisions—whether to get married, and to whom; whether to have children, and if so, when; what kind of job to take; where to live—are usually made by people who are at least 21 years old. Smoking is one of those major life decisions that people tend to make much earlier. In fact, according to the American Lung Association, deciding whether or not to smoke is basically a teenage decision. "Tobacco use primarily begins in early adolescence, typically by age 16," says the ALA. "[A]lmost all first use occurs before the time of high school graduation."

So if you're deciding whether or not to smoke, this might be one of the biggest decisions you've made yet. How do you choose?

Let's start with the basics: Why does *anyone* choose to smoke? Here's a list of some reasons. Can you think of others?

Why Smoke?

- My family does.
- My friends do.

- It looks cool, sexy, tough, or some other way I want to be.
- It's *my* decision—my parents, teachers, and other grown-ups can't tell me what to do.
- It gives me something to do with my hands.
- It gives me a way to start conversations or to hang out with people more comfortably.
- It perks me up.
- It relaxes me.
- It helps me concentrate.
- I'd like to try it out for myself—I can always quit later.
- It's hard to say no when people offer it to me.
- I'm afraid that if I don't say yes, I'll lose my friends, or at the very least, stand out way too much.
- It helps me keep my weight down.

Would it surprise you to learn that being in a family whose members smoke is probably the best predictor of whether or not a teenager will smoke? That's the opinion of youth worker and sociologist Mike Males. He writes:

All teenagers are exposed to the $6 billion per year tobacco advertising barrage [as of 1996, when he was writing], though only a fraction smoke. All teenagers are exposed to "peer pressure," though only a fraction seem to take it seriously. All teenagers are exposed to their own teenagerness. What, then, makes the fraction which smokes different from the majority that seems well able to resist these universal "pressures"?

There is no one answer; even studies that investigate a variety of factors still find that the biggest motivators are individual. But the largest, most logical, most research-pinpointed (and most never-mentioned-by-health-officials) reason for youth smoking appears to be smoking by adults, itself a complex phenomenon. Teen smoking is highly concentrated among certain demographic subgroups—low income, mostly white and Hispanic youths from backgrounds in which adults smoke. Among 26–34-year-olds, 53 percent of those with less than a high school education, and

37 percent of those with a high school diploma but no college (that is, the low-income group) are smokers. This is the prime age group raising kids on housefuls of airborne Carolina carcinogen, and this is indeed the demographic group where most adolescent smokers are found as well—another coincidence!

Males includes the following chart to show that teenage smoking mirrors adult smoking in pretty much every measurable way. The only exception were African-American teens, who in 1993, when the figures were collected, smoked at far lower rates than African-American adults. (Since then, as we've seen, the smoking rates for black teenagers, especially boys, has gone up, along with the smoking rate for African-American adults.)

Teens Smoke Like the Adults of Their Sex, Race, Locale			
Monthly Smoking*	Age 12–17	Age 18–34	Ratio Youth-Adult
Males	9.3%	31.2%	.30
Females	10.0	28.1	.36
Whites	11.0	31.8	.35
Blacks	4.0	23.9	.17
Hispanics	8.4	25.1	.33
Other	10.1	23.6	.43
Large metro	8.1	26.1	.31
Small metro	12.0	30.4	.39
Nonmetro	9.1	36.8	.25
Northeast	10.5	31.6	.33
North Central	11.1	29.1	.38
South	8.4	30.8	.27
West	9.0	26.4	.34
All	9.6%	29.6%	.32

* Data from 1993.

Sources: U.S. Substance Abuse and Mental Health Services Administration. *National Household Survey on Drug Abuse: Population Estimates 1993* (Tables 1A–14H). Washington, D.C.: U.S. Department of Health and Human Services, 1994.

Males also cites a 1993 Los Angeles survey of student smoking that he himself conducted. Of 407 teenagers surveyed, 46.1 percent of those who had at least one smoking parent had tried cigarettes, whereas only 28.2 percent of those with no smoking parents had experimented with tobacco. Some 16.3 percent of those with smoking parents were themselves smoking weekly or even daily by age 15, compared to only 5.6 percent of those with nonsmoking parents. And 13.8 percent of those who smoked weekly or daily by age 13 had one or more smoking parents, as opposed only 3.8 percent of those whose parent did not smoke.

Even with one or more smoking parents, some 50.3 percent of the teens said they were nonsmokers and planned never to smoke. But of those whose parents did not smoke, the percentage of kids who "didn't smoke and didn't plan to" rose to 71.8 percent. Males figured the odds from these results and concluded that smoking parents were three times more likely to have smoking kids.

Although it's dangerous to rely on anecdotes for large statistical questions, here's a quote from one nonsmoking 29-year-old who emphatically agreed with the theory of parental influence on smoking: "Oh, clearly, parents' smoking is the main factor in a kid's decision. My parents were strongly against smoking, and my brother and I wanted to please them, so we didn't smoke. My sister, on the other hand, was a rebel, so she did smoke. She made a different decision from me and my brother—but we were all basing our decision on our parents."

Which do *you* think is more important—friends or family? While Males makes a convincing case that your parents' behavior on smoking is most likely to determine yours, there are some experts who believe that friends who smoke are even more influential than parents are. "Peers, siblings, and friends are powerful influences," says the American

Lung Association. "The most common situation for first trying a cigarette is with a friend who already smokes."

Whether friends or family are more important, of course, in the end, the person who makes the final decision to smoke is *you*. So remember to put yourself first as you make this important decision.

Why Do People Choose Not to Smoke?

OK, we've looked at the pros. Now let's look at the cons. Why don't people smoke?

Here's a list of some reasons. What can you add?

Why Avoid Smoking?

- I'm concerned about my health in the long term: I don't want to get lung cancer, emphysema, heart disease, or any of the other smoking-related illnesses that long-term smokers get.
- I'm concerned about my health in the short term: I don't want to have shortness of breath, sore throats, teeth and gum problems, higher blood pressure, or any of the other smoking-related problems that teenagers get.
- I'm an athlete, and smoking hurts my performance.
- I'm a dancer, and smoking hurts my performance.
- I'm an actor, a singer, or a public speaker, and smoking is bad for my voice.
- I don't like the smell or the taste.
- I don't like the way it makes me smell.
- My boyfriend/girlfriend doesn't like the taste or smell.
- I don't like the image.
- I don't like the people I know who smoke.
- I'm concerned about what smoking does to my skin.
- I don't like the way it turns my teeth yellow or brown.
- I'm afraid I couldn't quit.

- I don't like being dependent on something.
- I don't want to spend the money.
- I don't like being manipulated by the tobacco companies.
- I'm afraid if I started smoking and then quit, I'd gain weight.

Now let's look at some of the facts behind both the pro- and the anti-smoking lists.

Smoking and Health

We've said it before, but it bears repeating: Each day, 3,000 people in the United States between the ages of 12 and 20 smoke their first cigarette. Most of those people are under 18. And 1,000 of them will end up dead because of smoking.

Following are some other health-related facts about smoking that everyone should know

- Smoking keeps teenagers' lungs from functioning as well as they otherwise might and makes it harder for teenagers to exercise. Girls feel this restriction even more than boys.
- Teenage smokers suffer from shortness of breath almost three times as often as nonsmoking teens.
- The earlier you start smoking, the greater your risk of lung cancer.
- Almost 23 million American women smoke. And women age 35 or older are 12 times more likely to have an early death from smoking than women who don't smoke. Because of smoking, lung cancer has now outpaced breast cancer as the most common form of cancer among U.S. women. In 1994, 57,589 American women died of lung cancer, compared to 43,644 who died of breast cancer.

"I Can Always Quit"

Most teens who start smoking plan to quit—but most find that they can't. In this way, they're a lot like the adults who smoke: Most of them want to quit, but they can't do it, either. That's because it's *hard* to quit smoking. We'll talk more about quitting—and ways to help yourself quit—in Chapter 5.

For now, let's just review the statistics.

- Some 46 million adults in the United States smoke, and most of them wish they could quit.
- More than 90 percent of young people who use either cigarettes or smokeless tobacco every day had at least one symptom of withdrawal when they tried to quit.
- Teenagers can become addicted by smoking only one cigarette a day.
- Some 75 percent of the young people who smoke or chew tobacco each day report that "It's really hard to quit."
- Two-thirds of young smokers say they want to quit, and 70 percent say that they would not start smoking if they could choose again.
- Of the teenagers who have smoked at least 100 cigarettes in their lifetime, most say that they'd like to quit—but can't.
- People who start smoking early are more likely to be more addicted to nicotine than those who start later.

Cigarettes and Weight

One of the most common reasons given for either starting smoking or continuing to smoke is because of weight. It's true that people who start smoking tend to lose weight and go on to gain weight more slowly than nonsmokers. And because the effect continues, smokers tend to weigh 7 pounds less than nonsmokers. It's also true that people who quit smoking may suddenly gain weight—an average of 6 pounds in the year that they stop.

This effect on weight is apparently the work of nicotine, since nicotine gum also slows weight gain. Although smoking does depress the appetite, studies show that smokers eat at least as much as nonsmokers, so nicotine's real effect is in the *metabolism*, the way our bodies process food. Even though smokers tend to be less physically active than nonsmokers, nicotine apparently helps the body process food at a higher rate if it enters the system while the smoker or snuff-taker is mildly active.

In other words, if a smoker *only* smokes when he or she is fully relaxed—as, say, Vanessa's mother tends to do—the nicotine probably won't affect his or her metabolism so dramatically. But if a smoker or snuff-taker is walking, working, or engaged in some other mild activity while taking in nicotine, the nicotine bumps up metabolism and makes it harder to gain weight.

Women seem to be more affected in this way than men are—and they're certainly more concerned about their weight than men are. Studies have shown that women are more likely to overestimate their weight than men are and less likely to be accurate about just how heavy or slim they really are. Studies have also shown that women are more likely to give weight as a reason for smoking and are more likely to go back to smoking after quitting because of concerns about their weight.

Sadly, the use of cigarettes as a weight-loss tool is counterbalanced by the increased number of lung cancer–related deaths among women. Cigarette makers are well aware of girls' concerns about weight, and they target teenage girls with ads featuring ultraslim models. The campaigns seem to be working: A 1995 survey by the Centers for Disease Control and Prevention showed that 34.3% of high school girls smoke, and 15.9% smoke frequently.

If you're a teenage girl who's thinking about smoking as a way to keep your weight down, please make this decision very carefully. There are other ways to deal with the question of weight, but you have only one life to live and only one body to carry you through that life. Make sure that the choice you make about smoking is one that will help you stay alive and healthy, with a body you can enjoy for many years to come.

Smoking and Pregnancy

Any young woman who's planning on getting pregnant should certainly stop and consider the effects of smoking on an unborn child. Smoking during pregnancy accounts for an estimated 20 percent to 30 percent of low-birthweight babies, who have a lower chance of survival and are susceptible to many more illnesses and problems than babies of average birth weight. Smoking is also linked to as many as 14 percent of preterm deliveries, or deliveries of babies before the full nine months of pregnancy, which again, puts the babies at higher risk. Indeed, some 10 percent of all infant deaths are tied to smoking.

A girl or woman who smokes now might tell herself that she'll quit when she gets pregnant. But that's often hard to do, and studies show that just cutting back on smoking might not benefit the baby. People who smoke less, or who switch to low-tar cigarettes, tend to inhale more deeply in order to get the amount of nicotine they're used to. They may be taking fewer drags or smoking a different brand, but the baby can't tell the difference.

Who's Calling the Shots?

Let's be blunt: Tobacco companies need new smokers. Why? Because the older ones die. If the industry is to keep sales at the same level, let alone increase them, it has to recruit new smokers. And the best place to find new smokers is among young people, since, as we've seen, most people decide whether or not to smoke when they're still teenagers.

Another good place to find new smokers is among sectors of the population where smoking rates may not be as high as among others: for example, women, African Americans, and Latinos. According to the American Lung Association, "As smoking has declined among the White non-Hispanic population, tobacco companies have targeted both African Americans and Hispanics with intensive merchandising, which includes billboards, advertising in media oriented to those communities, and sponsorship of civil groups and athletic, cultural, and entertainment events."

Here's the current breakdown of smoking by ethnic group, according to the ALA:

Group	Percent Who Smoke
Native Americans/Alaskan Natives	42.2
Latinos	29.5
African Americans	27.2
Whites	26.3
Asians and Pacific Islanders	13.9

The third target market for the smokeless tobacco and cigarette industry is poor people, who, as Mike Males has pointed out, are far more likely to smoke than middle- and upper-income people.

Often, of course, these groups overlap. And the tobacco industry is not shy about playing on the fears and insecurities of the people who turn to cigarettes. As early as 1973, Claude E. Teague Jr., assistant director of research and development at R.J. Reynolds, wrote, "The fragile, developing self-image of the young person needs all of the support and enhancement it can get."

In 1975, the Ted Bates ad agency for Brown & Williamson (the tobacco company later bought by the British

American Tobacco Company), pointed out that for most young smokers, cigarettes were not yet a normal part of their routine but that the teen smokers tried to make it look as if it were. The agency found that most teenagers associated cigarettes in a positive way with other "adult" activities, such as drinking alcohol, having sex, and taking drugs. "Having observed these parallels," explained one of the cigarette company "secret documents," "the report recommends positioning Viceroy [a cigarette brand] in the youth market by linking the brand to illicit coming-of-age activities."

As we've seen, tobacco companies try to develop a friendly relationship with the youth market by offering free gifts: key chains, sports bags, and other products emblazoned with a cigarette brand logo. If you've gotten these kinds of products, you can decide if the cigarette companies are really giving you something for nothing or if they are hoping to get something very important from you in return.

Deciding to Decide

Are you still trying to decide about whether or not to start or continue smoking? If so, here's one way you might make the decision.

- Take two sheets of paper. On one, write "Reasons to Smoke." Under that heading, write every single reason you can think of. Don't judge anything you write, just keep your pen moving. In order to make a good decision, you need to be aware of your thoughts and feelings, and this process will help you do that.
- On the second sheet of paper, write "Reasons Not to Smoke." Now write everything you can think of, again, without stopping to judge yourself or your reasoning. For now, just express yourself.
- When you're done with your two lists, take a third sheet of paper. Write at the top "How This Decision Makes Me

Feel." For at least five minutes, write without stopping, just jotting down whatever comes to mind. You may find yourself writing disconnected words or complete sentences or some combination of the two. It doesn't matter. This is for your eyes only. Just write.

- Just making your two lists and writing for a while may help you come to a decision. But if you haven't decided yet, look at each list, slowly and carefully. Ideally, you'd do this a few hours or even a day after you first started this process. Cross out any reason that you don't want to be guided by. Rate all the reasons that you do want to be guided by on a scale of 1 to 5, where 5 means "great reason—very important to me," and 1 means "not a very good reason—not very important to me."

- Add up the points for each side. Which comes to a bigger number?

- Look at the two scores. How do you feel? Do the numbers you've come up with reflect your true feelings about smoking? Do you feel a sense of relief that you've found your decision? Do you feel upset because you don't like the decision you're seeing? If you're still not satisfied, take yet another sheet of paper and try to write about why.

- Finally, if you still don't feel happy with what you've come up with, take one last sheet of paper and make one more list of "Things I Could Do to Help Me Decide." Jot down whatever comes to mind, and look at your list in a day or two. Sometimes the process of figuring out *how* to decide is the most important part of the decision.

Whatever you decide about smoking, remember: If you start smoking now, it's probably a decision that you'll have to live with for quite a long time, perhaps for the rest of your life. So make sure you choose a decision you can live with, one whose consequences you will be happy to accept.

And, if you've decided to quit smoking, or if you'd like to know more about what quitting smoking is like, turn to the next chapter.

5

Making Decisions
About Quitting

Angelica goes through the same decision-making
process about whether or not to smoke that was
described in the previous chapter. For a while, it's tough
because she rates "being like my friend, Lynette" and
"fitting in with Lynette's crowd" as 5s—factors that are
very important to her.

Finally, though, Angelica decides that one other factor is
even more important to her: not being dependent on
something outside her body to make herself feel better. She
doesn't like the idea of being addicted to cigarettes; it makes
her feel as though the cigarettes, not she, are in control.

Angelica also realizes that one thing she *doesn't* like
about watching Lynette smoke is seeing how desperate her
friend gets for a cigarette. For example, once Angelica and
Lynette were taking the bus to the mall, and there was an
unusual amount of traffic. The bus took almost half an hour
longer than usual to reach their stop, and by then, Lynette
was almost jumping out of her skin. She had a cigarette in
her mouth before they even got off the bus, and she was

lighting it the minute her feet hit the pavement. Angelica doesn't like the thought that anything could make her feel that crazy and out of control.

Clarence goes through his own decision-making process about whether or not to quit smoking. He makes two lists, one of the *pros* and the other of the *cons*. On the *con* side, against quitting, are reasons such as "how much I like cigarettes," "how awful it will feel to quit," and "just because everybody says they're bad for me doesn't mean they are." On the *pro* side, for quitting, are other reasons such as "I don't like the cigarette companies pushing me around," "I don't like thinking I can't do something," and "I've noticed I'm smoking more and more, and that bugs me."

Clarence might have spent several weeks going back and forth, continuing to smoke while debating whether to quit. What finally leads him to a decision, however, is another factor that he had never expected: He gets involved with someone who *isn't* a smoker, and that person doesn't like the way cigarettes make Clarence taste. The idea of never kissing his new love is even worse than the idea of never having another cigarette, so Clarence decides to quit.

Vanessa prepares carefully for her talk with her parents. She thinks about talking to both of them together, but then she realizes that it will be easier to talk to her mother first. If she can make some headway with her mom, maybe her mom can help her talk to her dad, or even do the talking for her.

So Vanessa thinks hard about what she might say or do that would appeal to her mother. She makes the following list of the first ideas that come to mind:

1. Offer to do the dishes and mop the kitchen floor every night if you won't smoke.
2. It's hurting my voice and I won't do well in the play.
3. My throat is sore *all the time.*

4. I worry about your health—I don't want *you* to get sick and die!
5. I hate the smell!
6. It makes me mad that you get to smoke, and there are all these things that are bad for me that *I'm* not supposed to do.

Vanessa decides that point 1 is unrealistic because she really doesn't want to do all that work. She thinks that 5 and 6 will probably make her mother mad, which won't help her case. However, 2, 3 and 4 might make her mother stop and think.

Vanessa also looks at the lists of compromises she's made. She decides she'll start by asking her mother if they can agree on two things: no smoking at the dinner table, and no smoking on the second floor, where the bedrooms are. That way, Vanessa won't be exposed to smoke during dinner and in her own room. If her parents want to keep smoking—even though Vanessa wishes they wouldn't—they can. But at least Vanessa's health will be a bit more protected.

Who Wants to Quit?

If you look around, at the people in your life and the ads in your world, you can probably identify lots of smokers. But do you know anyone who has quit or anyone who wants to quit? Ex-smokers and would-be ex-smokers are harder to spot than people who currently smoke—but their thoughts, feelings, and experiences have a lot to teach us.

In 1994, some 46 million adults were *former* smokers. That's 26 million men and 20 million women, adding up to $1/4$ of the total U.S. population. Of the people who were still smoking in 1994, 33.2 million said they wanted to quit completely. That's about 69 percent, or more than $2/3$, of current smokers.

That 69 percent might have *wanted* to quit, but according to the American Cancer Society, they were finding it difficult. "Quit attempts," writes the Cancer Society, "abstaining from smoking for at least one day during the preceding 12 months [before 1994], were made by about 46% of current every-day smokers." But since the rate of smoking didn't fall 46 percent between 1993 and 1994, we can assume that a large portion of these attempts did not succeed.

Why Do People Want to Quit?

As Angelica, Clarence, and Vanessa's stories remind us, the reasons people have for quitting are as varied as people themselves. Here are some known reasons. Can you think of others?

Why Quit Smoking?

- I'm worried about dying—from lung cancer, emphysema, heart disease, other cancers.
- I'm worried about getting sick—from bronchitis, mouth cancer, throat cancer, cancer of the larynx, other diseases.
- I'm worried about my present health—shortness of breath, loss of stamina, voice problems.
- My boyfriend or girlfriend doesn't like the smell or taste.
- I'm hanging out with a new crowd where smoking isn't accepted.
- I'm tired of spending money on cigarettes.
- I don't like the feeling of being addicted.
- I'm mad at the tobacco companies.
- I've given up some other addiction (such as drinking or taking drugs), and it seemed important or necessary to stop smoking too.

- I know someone who got sick or died from a smoking-related disease.
- I'm worried about wrinkles, discolored teeth, gum problems, bad breath.

Supermodel Christy Turlington quit smoking in 1995, at age 26. Although Turlington had been smoking since she was 13, she stopped cold turkey because her father died from lung cancer. She gives some other reasons, too, for quitting in three public service announcements she made for the American Cancer Society. (You may have seen them; they ran on MTV.) "I see someone smoking and I think they're out of control," Turlington said, explaining why she wanted to make the ads. "I smoked a pack a day for years. It wasn't fabulous or gorgeous—I was addicted."

In one ad, "Smoking Can Alter Your Good Looks," Turlington is shown on time-lapse video going from her current fabulous state to someone with wrinkled skin, discolored teeth and nails, and dried-out hair. "Smoking can give you looks that kill," she says. "I am glad I quit."

In the second ad, "Smoking Doesn't Make You Successful," the viewer sees artistic people, models, and socialites getting older and looking sadder as they smoke. "Fact is, you can alter photographs, but you can't hide the truth. Smoking is not glamorous. Smoking is a disease," Turlington says.

The third ad, "Smoking Is a Choice," shows Turlington doing a number of stylish things. "I chose to smoke," she says. "I chose to wake up each morning coughing. I chose to fill my body with tar. I chose to breathe a little less each time I reached for a cigarette. Then, I chose to quit."

Another famous ex-smoker is Patrick Reynolds, the grandson of cigarette tycoon R. J. Reynolds. Although Reynolds's family has made a fortune in the tobacco business, he became an antismoking crusader after watching most of his family die from smoking.

"This is a personal mission for me," said Reynolds on an April 18, 1998, edition of the PBS program *Adam Smith's Money Game.* "My father died from smoking when I was 15. My grandfather probably died from chewing tobacco. My oldest brother, R. J. Reynolds III, died from smoking. My Aunt Nancy died from smoking. Aunt Mary smoked and died from cancer. My mother smoked and got an aneurysm [an often-fatal blood clot that can interefere with the brain]. Smoking has decimated my family."

According to *Money World* correspondent Adele Malpass, "Reynolds claims the turning point was the pain of watching both his parents die. He says it was especially hard at age 15 to watch his father die from smoking after having an active life. In 1979 Patrick Reynolds took the big step. He sold all his tobacco stock worth millions."

"There I am, an [addicted] smoker," Reynolds explained on the show, "and I've got a cigarette in one hand [on the show, Reynolds pretends to be smoking] and the telephone in the other hand and saying, 'Look, I don't want to own the Reynolds stock. Sell it!' And the broker said, 'Mr. Reynolds, there'll be capital gains [a type of high tax] to pay on that.' And then I said, 'I don't care. Sell the tobacco stock. I don't like being a cigarette addict. I just want to get rid of it.'" Although Reynolds's stock would be worth even more today, he says he has no regrets—he just wants to work to create "a smoke-free society in the 21st Century."

Quitting and Your Health

One of the main reasons that people quit—or wish that their loved ones would quit—is to protect their health. Although the health hazards of smoking are serious and long lasting, the health benefits of quitting kick in almost immediately.

- People who quit, no matter how old they are, live longer than people who continue to smoke.
- Smokers who quit before age 50 have half the risk of dying in the next 15 years, compared with those who keep smoking.
- Quitting smoking substantially lowers the chance of getting many different types of cancer: of the lung, larynx, esophagus, mouth, pancreas, bladder, and cervix.
- If you quit, you've got a lot less chance of getting some other major disease, including coronary heart disease and cardiovascular disease.

Now at this point, you might be thinking, "OK, great. Smoking may be bad for my health, but I don't have to worry about getting cancer or heart disease for years to come. By the time it's a problem, I can just quit!"

Don't kid yourself. It gets much, *much* harder to quit the longer you've smoked. Remember the explanation in Chapter 3 of how smoking starts your heart racing first thing in the morning? Well, the longer you've depended on smoking to do that for you, the harder it is to do it for yourself. So longtime smokers feel much worse when they quit than people who've been smoking for only a few months or a few years.

Likewise, remember the discussion in Chapter 3 of how smoking helps relax you by blocking the action of stress chemicals on the nicotinic receptors in your body? Well, once again, as your body gets used to the aid of nicotine, it compensates by doing less for itself. You were born with some natural chemicals inside you to help calm you down—one of them is *dopamine*—and these natural "downers" have their own receptor sites in your brain. If nicotine is doing their job, however, your body doesn't want to get *too* relaxed. So it starts making less dopamine and shutting down some of the dopamine receptor sites. Then you stop smoking, and all of a sudden neither nicotine *nor* dopamine is blocking those stress messages. It's no wonder that smokers feel so stressed out when they quit. But the less time they've been smoking, the more natural chemicals their body has in reserve and the more quickly the body can bounce back to making its own de-stress drugs.

Here are some of the other longer-term health benefits of quitting smoking.

- Smoking takes an average of at least seven years off every smoker's life, which works out to five and a half minutes per cigarette. So every cigarette that you *don't* smoke might buy you a little more time.
- The risk of heart attack returns to normal after five years of not smoking, no matter how long you've smoked.
- The risk of lung cancer drops considerably after five years of not smoking.
- People with emphysema who have smoked still lose some of their breathing capacity—but the rate of loss goes way down once they've stopped smoking.
- Even people in their 60s who have lots of smoking-related problems live longer if they stop smoking.

If you're a smoker in your 40s, 50s, or 60s, you might be glad to read these statistics. "Wow," you can tell yourself. "Even though I've been smoking for so many years, if I stop smoking now, my body can eventually get some of its health back." If you're a teenage smoker, though, these statistics might be rather depressing: Look how many years it's going to take your body to get back to normal if you continue to smoke! And of course, if you get cancer, heart disease, or some other illness *before* you stop smoking, you're dealing with a serious health problem whether you quit or not.

In other words, if you're already smoking, the way to beat the odds is to stop now. Because the sooner you stop, the sooner the healing time can begin.

To Quit or Not to Quit?

If you're having trouble deciding whether or not to quit, you might take a look at the section on decision making in Chapter 4. Here's a modified version of the process described there that you can use to help you make your decision.

- Take two sheets of paper. At the top of one write "Reasons to Keep Smoking." Under that heading, write every single reason you can think of. Don't judge anything you write, just keep your pen moving. In order to make a good decision, you need to be aware of your thoughts and feelings, and this process will help you do that.
- On the second sheet of paper, write "Reasons to Quit." Again, write everything you can think of without stopping to judge yourself or your reasoning. For now, just express yourself.
- When you're done with your two lists, take a third sheet of paper. Write at the top "How This Decision Makes Me Feel." For at least five minutes, write without stopping, just jotting down whatever comes to mind. You may find yourself writing disconnected words or complete sentences or some combination of the two. It doesn't matter. This is for your eyes only. Just write.
- If after doing this your decision still isn't clear to you, or if you're still not satisfied with it, put the pages away for a day or two. Then look at each list, slowly and carefully. Cross out any reason that you don't want to use in making an important decision. Rate the reasons that remain on a scale of 1 to 5, where *5* means "great reason—very important to me," and *1* means "not a very good reason—not very important to me."
- Add up the points for each side. Which comes to a bigger number?

- Look at the two scores. Does a decision feel clear to you yet? Do you feel relieved, upset, anxious, scared, proud, happy, uncertain? Sometimes even the right decision will feel upsetting, but if you look deep within yourself, you can usually tell if it's right. Give yourself some quiet time to listen to what your mind, body, and feelings are telling you.

If you do decide to quit, hold on to these pages. Highlight the parts that you feel most strongly about and post them in your room, tape them in your notebook, or put them somewhere else where you can go back to them again and again, any time you need a reminder of why you want to quit.

If you decide not to quit, you might still want to hang on to the pages where you've recorded your decision-making process. Someday you might want to come back and look at them again, if only to remind yourself of how you once felt.

What It's Like to Quit

As we've seen, the good news about quitting is that you've taken an important step to safeguard your health. Some other good news: Any smoking-related problems you've been having with your skin, hair, and teeth start to reverse. If you've been having shortness of breath, sore throats, smoker's cough, problems with your voice, or any other symptom of smoking, it will go away fairly soon after you stop. This is true for all smokers, but especially true of teenage smokers and users of smokeless tobacco, who haven't been smoking or chewing as long as adult users.

Of course, the bad news is that quitting can be painful and unpleasant. As we just saw, your body has gotten used to nicotine to help rev it up and calm it down. When you take that nicotine away, your body screams in protest. Obviously you *can* get through the hard times—lots of people have. But here's what you should be prepared for.

Many smokers experience feelings of craving, tension, irritability, restlessness, depression, and difficulty in concentrating. The degree to which these symptoms apply to you is pretty directly related to the amount of nicotine you've been taking in—either smoking or dipping snuff—before you quit. Usually, these symptoms last about a week. Sometimes they are very mild; sometimes people don't have any symptoms at all.

Some people, especially long-term smokers, experience more intense reactions, according to John Fahs. Fahs, a former longtime smoker, writes:

> It's been over four years since I stopped smoking. For the first twenty-eight days, I knew I was losing my mind, but didn't link the taste of stark-raving insanity I'd become resigned to, to quitting nicotine. The revelation didn't come until I ran into my friend Heather, who'd also just quit (ironically, on the same day I did) and was experiencing similar symptoms: auditory and visual hallucinations, ranging from severe to mild; periods of total blackout lasting up for forty-five minutes, bottomless rage, and a host of other odd symptoms.

Fahs, who was inspired to stop smoking by watching his father die of lung cancer, believes that his reactions were caused by the additives and increased nicotine content that have allegedly characterized cigarettes in recent years. He says that most of the scientific literature on quitting smoking was collected in an earlier era, when cigarettes were not quite as potent as they have since become.

Here are some of the physical changes that will be going on in your body as you quit smoking. Again, the longer you've smoked, the more intense these symptoms are likely to be.

- slower pulse
- drop in blood pressure
- occasional constipation

- occasional drop in the ability to perform difficult tasks and loss of concentration and/or patience
- dizziness
- tingling in the arms and legs
- coughing

It's interesting to relate these changes to what we know about the effects of nicotine on the body. Without the boost from nicotine, your heart beats a little slower for a while, hence the drop in pulse and blood pressure. If the studies showing that nicotine raises concentration and lowers aggression are valid, it makes sense that you'd temporarily lose these benefits when you stop smoking. The other possibility—that nicotine provides no absolute benefits, but quitting nicotine brings on temporary losses—would also explain this effect. The dizziness is because without smoking, more oxygen is getting to your brain and you're just not used to it yet. (Take heart. Once you *are* used to it, that extra oxygen will make you feel great!) The coughing is your body trying to get rid of all the smoking-related chemicals that are still in your system.

"Hundreds of Times"

Have you ever heard Mark Twain's famous joke about kicking the smoking habit? "Quitting smoking isn't hard at all," the famous humorist is supposed to have said. "Why, I've done it hundreds of times!"

The puzzle of why people go back to smoking after they've gone through the difficulties of quitting continues to baffle scientists. After all, once the nicotine is out of your body, which can happen within a month, there's no *physical* reason to resume. Yet when the American Health Foundation questioned 500 smokers who had quit, they found that after 1 month, only 30 percent had continued to stay away from smoking, and after 1 year, the figure had dropped to 20 percent, which seems to be the average success rate for quitting across a number of studies. What makes staying away so difficult?

Nobody has a definitive answer, and as with most aspects of smoking, a lot of individual factors come into play. But David Krogh, who has looked at smoking from the point of view of trying to understand addiction, has two helpful thoughts on the matter.

First, he suggests, it's hard to stay away from cigarettes for the same reason that it's hard to quit: because cigarettes are linked to so many parts of a smoker's daily life. (Clarence discovered this as soon as he started even thinking about quitting.) People who are trying to stop drinking are counseled to change the parts of their life that they associate with drinking: not to go into bars, for example, or to stay away from the kinds of parties where they used to like to get drunk. Likewise, people who are trying to quit heroin are told to avoid the friends and companions that they used to get high with, since these reminders of past addiction are extremely powerful.

For smokers, however, it is more complicated than severing ties with one specific activity or group of people. Most smokers have found ways of integrating cigarettes into virtually every facet of their life—that's part of why smoking is so widespread. Clarence, for instance, smoked when he studied to help him concentrate; when he waited for a meal to ease his hunger; when he finished a meal to help him digest; when he needed to rev himself up for a difficult task; and when he wanted to calm himself down to get ready for bed. He could hardly avoid all of these situations—and every single one of them made him want a cigarette.

Krogh's other notion is related to the first: He suggests that cigarette smokers, along with heroin addicts, alcoholics, and others who become addicted to various substances and behaviors, simply miss the good feelings that the drug or behavior brought on. Sure, your mind knows that smoking can kill you, and your body might even know that you feel a lot better being able to breathe deeply. But if you've smoked for a while, even after quitting you may continue to carry the memory of how good it felt to take that first cigarette of the day or how nice it was to take a midday smoking break.

John Fahs recounts that even after he stopped smoking, he continued to miss cigarettes the way he might miss a former lover. ". . . deep down I still loved cigarettes. I pined for them and [for] the unrequited love affair I'd indulged in since adolescence, the kind of unquestioning, unconditional love often lavished on scornful partners."

Even though it may not be possible to cut every association with cigarettes or chewing tobacco out of your life, knowing that these associations are powerful can help you quit smoking or chewing—and stay "quit." To find out how, take a look at the next section.

One Day at a Time: Tips to Help You Quit

This section is named "One Day at a Time" after the powerful slogan associated with Alcoholics Anonymous, a group that has helped hundreds of thousands of people stop drinking. AA wisdom has it that if you picture your whole life without another drink—or another cigarette—the prospect is just too daunting. No one can imagine giving up so much without at least a twinge of regret or maybe a full-blown feeling of "I can't do it," But, the advice goes, if you just focus on the present, on getting through the next day, the next hour, the next minute, that you can do.

Such advice is especially useful for people who have quit and are feeling tempted to start again. Research shows that if you're an ex-smoker, you may feel longings for a cigarette for up to at least nine years after you quit. Such cravings can be discouraging to the person who has gone through the difficulties of quitting, but take heart. Research also shows that these feelings last only about three to five minutes. While you're in the midst of a craving, it might *seem* as though it's going to last forever. But if you know better, you can use that knowledge to hold out past the craving.

With that in mind, here are some suggestions that can help you stop smoking.

- *Be aware that different methods work for different people.* Shop around: Ask people you know how *they* quit, or call up one of the groups listed in Chapter 7 and find out what techniques are available. And be persistent. If nicotine gum won't work for you, maybe the nicotine patch will. Maybe you're the kind of person who does better quitting on your own, or perhaps you're the sort who does better with group support. Try to look at the process of quitting as something you're learning how to do, not something you get one chance to succeed or fail at.
- *Keep trying.* Most smokers try to quit and fail several times. If you have this experience, you're not alone, and it doesn't mean you'll never succeed. In fact, says the Association for Nonsmokers' Rights, "There's some evidence that the more times a smoker has tried and failed to quit, the better the chance of success the next time."
- *Pick the right time to quit.* If you're totally psyched and ready to go, then that *is* the right time, no matter what else is going on. Go for it—and good luck! But if you've got more leeway, choose wisely. The week before a big test, right around holidays, or just as some major, stressful event is coming up is probably the worst possible time to quit. While there's never an ideal time, some times may be worse than others. Try to avoid them as you plan your quitting strategy.
- *Know* **why** *you want to quit.* You are your own best ally in the quitting process. Being clear about who you

are and what you want is the most powerful thing you can do for yourself. Go back to those lists you made, or make new lists. Write your reasons on index cards in beautiful colors and keep them in your pocket or bag, where you can reach for them instead of for a cigarette. Make up little rhymes or special sentences to remind you of what you want: "I love my body when I'm feeling strong" or "Long life, good life." (OK, you can probably do better than *that*. But you get the idea!)

- ***Know* how *you smoke.*** It might help to keep a smoking journal the week before you plan to quit, or at the very least, pay close attention to your smoking habits. Do you smoke at particular times of the day? Under particular circumstances? Which cigarettes taste great, and which do you smoke only out of habit? The more you know, the more you can "dance" with your habits, figuring out ways of substituting other activities or giving yourself other rewards instead of cigarettes.

- ***As the first step in the quitting process, lower the amount of nicotine in your system by using low-tar cigarettes.*** This point only applies to people who aren't already smoking the lowest possible rating of tar and nicotine. Otherwise, look at your own brand's rating. In your first week, buy a brand that's lower in tar by 30 percent; then, in your second week, cut back by 60 percent; and in your third week, by 90 percent. Even though it's true that you may compensate by smoking more deeply, you probably will be cutting back at least some of the nicotine in your system, which should make actual quitting easier. And the process will probably make you more conscious of smoking, which is also helpful.

- ***Go cold turkey.*** When you're done "fading out" the nicotine by using low-tar cigarettes, stop completely. What you want to avoid is a situation where you're dying for a smoke and you have to decide whether or not you get to have one. Knowing that you can't, while harder in the short run, makes it easier to really quit in the long run. Otherwise, your life becomes one long bargaining process with cigarettes (or chewing tobacco)—and tobacco becomes *more* important in your life, not less.

- ***Vary your routine.*** Remember when we talked about cigarettes (and chewing tobacco) being connected with pretty much every moment of a smoker's life? Well, you can't change your entire life, but you can vary it. If you smoke while doing the crossword puzzle, for instance, maybe you could work the puzzle sitting outside on the front step, rather than curled up in your favorite chair. If you smoke after dinner, maybe you could plan a brisk after-dinner walk downtown for some ice cream—or for a frozen-fruit popsicle, if you're worried about your weight. If you smoke as soon as you get off the bus, maybe you could get off a stop earlier. Be playful; be creative. Think of your smoking self as a person you don't want to run into for a while. What can you do to throw that smoking self "off the scent"?

- ***Find something else to put into your mouth.*** Sugarless gum, carrot and celery sticks, or dietetic candy might be good substitutes for tobacco products, and unwrapping/eating them gives you something to do with your hands too. Obviously, you don't want to be loading yourself up with sweets. Aside from the potential weight gain and dental problems, the sugar will make you jumpy, and that's the last thing you need. But giving yourself *some* substitute for putting a cigarette in your mouth might help.

- ***Take up exercise.*** If you're already an athlete, you might turn to the kind of physical activity you already enjoy. If you're more the couch-potato type, now's your chance to get physical. Martial arts—tai chi, karate, aikido—and yoga are especially good anticigarette aids, because they emphasize connections between mind and body, rely on deep breathing, and tend to improve concentration and focus. If you start the day with some kind of aerobic exercise or another type of deep breathing, that will rev up your heart and clear your head the way nicotine used to. And if you associate learning a new physical skill with giving up smoking, the more you practice that skill, the more positive reinforcement you'll have for staying away from tobacco.

- *Eat wisely.* This is hardly the time to go on a diet, but remember that sugar, caffeine, and high-fat foods can make you feel jumpy, irritable, and sluggish. Fresh fruit and vegetables, high-fiber carbohydrates (brown rice, whole wheat bread), and lean protein (skinless chicken and turkey, fish) can help clean out your system. Dairy products (milk, cheese, yogurt) help produce mucus, so if you're coughing a lot, ease up on these for a while. Some people claim that a moderate supplement of vitamin C helps with your breathing, while B vitamins are good for combating stress. (Too much vitamin B can also be dangerous, so don't take more than one B-complex vitamin a day.)

- *Get help if you need it.* You can find low-cost or free programs, which usually combine lectures, behavior management techniques, and peer support, through a local hospital, the American Lung Association, or the American Cancer Society. (See Chapter 7).

- *Consider the nicotine patch or nicotine gum.* Some nicotine products require a doctor's prescription; most nicotine gums don't. However, you probably should work with a doctor or at least consult your pharmacist about the most effective way to use these products. For example, it's important to use these products regularly if they're going to work for you. And you should know that the nicotine in gum enters your bloodstream through your mouth, not your stomach, so swallowing it will probably make you sick and won't help reduce your craving.

- *Get support from the people in your life.* Most people do better when their loved ones are supporting them.

Think of friends or family members that you trust, decide how they can best support you, and then ask for their help. That might range from asking them to offer you sticks of gum every so often to requesting their patience if you seem unusually grouchy or upset. You might also need to ask your smoking friends not to smoke when you're there, or to forgive your absence for the next few weeks or so, depending on how hard it is for you to be around other smokers as you yourself are trying to quit.

Does quitting now sound more manageable—or more difficult than ever? Either way, if this is the right decision for you, we urge you to keep at it and not give up until your body is smoke-free. You're not just gaining the physical benefits of giving up smoking. What you learn about yourself as you go through this process will stand you in good stead for the rest of your life.

6

Reaching Out
About Smoking

Angelica has been learning more and more about the health hazards associated with smoking. The more she finds out, the more she's starting to worry about the way Lynette uses cigarettes. But she's not sure what to do about her concerns. After all, smoking is Lynette's business, isn't it? She doesn't want Lynette to get mad at her. And she still thinks smoking has a cool side.

At the same time, Angelica thinks that friends should take care of each other, and she wants to make sure Lynette knows what she's risking by smoking so much. She's also a bit concerned about the dangers of secondhand smoke. If it were just Lynette, it wouldn't be so bad, but sometimes, after hanging out with Lynette's whole crowd of smoking friends, Angelica feels like a walking ashtray. "If I can smell the smoke on my clothes and in my hair," she thinks, "how much is actually going into my body?"

Now that Clarence has quit smoking, he can barely stand to be around other people who smoke. The first few weeks, he felt uncomfortable because he just wanted a cigarette so badly, and it was hard to watch other people enjoying a smoke when he couldn't. Now, though, he's having the opposite reaction: Cigarette smoke seems to make him sick to his stomach.

Clarence still likes the guys he used to hang out with when he was smoking—even though his new love interest, a nonsmoker, doesn't. Clarence knows it isn't as simple as who's a smoker and who isn't, but quitting smoking seems to have forced the issue. He feels bad about it, though, because he really doesn't want to lose all his old friends just because he's no longer smoking.

Vanessa tries talking to her mother, and although it doesn't go as well as she had hoped, it doesn't go too badly. At first, her mother just laughs and says, "You know, Vanessa, you can't always have everything your own way." Then she says, "You've got to remember, we're the grown-ups and you're the child. Your father and I are free to do what we want in our own house." Vanessa feels really angry that her mother isn't more concerned about things that matter to her, especially when it's a question of Vanessa's health.

Finally, though, Vanessa gets her mother to see that this is something she is really concerned about. Vanessa's mom agrees to bring up the idea of a no-smoking policy for the second floor of the house but warns Vanessa that her father probably won't go along with the idea of no smoking at mealtimes. Vanessa isn't satisfied, but it's a beginning. At least she said *something*.

Reaching Out to Friends

One of the most frustrating parts of making decisions is the way that other people sometimes react. Even though you've put a lot of thought, energy, and emotion into a decision that feels very important to you, the important people in your life don't always recognize that effort or agree with the conclusion you've come to.

This kind of gap often happens with smoking. Angelica might finally decide to say something to Lynette about smoking, purely out of concern for Lynette, only to have her friend react with anger, indifference, or even amusement. "Oh, you're just jealous because I've got a new crowd now," Lynette might say, and Angelica would have to wonder if maybe jealousy *is* part of the reason she's trying to get Lynette to quit smoking, or at least to consider quitting. Or Lynette might say, "Gee, what a baby. Just because you're not old enough to smoke, Angelica, doesn't mean that nobody is," and then Angelica would have to ask herself if she's really sure of her opinions about smoking, or if deep down, she thinks Lynette *is* more grown up and mature because she smokes.

On the other hand, *not* saying something about issues you feel strongly about has another kind of price. If Angelica is really concerned for her friend and doesn't say anything, she might feel guilty, nervous, or even angry at Lynette for causing her worry that she can't do anything about. She might never find out that Lynette has her own mixed feelings about smoking or that Lynette herself has been worrying about smoking too much. She might miss a chance to hear Lynette say, "I don't agree with anything you say, but I'm glad you care about me."

Of course, there's no way to know what Lynette's reaction will be unless Angelica actually talks to her. Angelica will have to decide whether or not talking to Lynette about this is worth the risk and then deal as best she can with the consequences or either saying or *not* saying something.

Likewise, Clarence is facing one of the hardest parts of being a teenager (and also, often, of being an adult): the gap that can grow between friends when their interests or patterns change. Getting a new boyfriend or girlfriend, becoming interested in new activities, stopping or starting a pattern of drug or alcohol use, all of these things can pull friends apart. Because people's interests change faster while they're teenagers than at any other time of life, teens probably face more "growing apart" times than either children or adults do.

Like Lynette, Clarence has some options. He can decide that he'll miss his old friends but that the change is really for the best. He can decide that he really wants to stay connected with them, and he's willing to give up both his new love and his new nonsmoking status to be closer to them. He can try to find ways of meeting in the middle, figuring out times that he can see his friends without his new love interest, or arranging activities that both the old and the new people in his life might enjoy together. He might negotiate with his friends, asking them not to smoke while they're out with him, or asking them to step outside to smoke, or offering to step outside himself.

None of this negotiation is easy, and like Angelica, Clarence risks a lot of bad reactions as well as having the potential for a lot of good ones. Clarence might end up feeling embarrassed, insulted, hurt, left out, or awkward. His friends might react with anger, annoyance, indifference, amusement, or scorn. On the other hand, Clarence and his friends might find new ways of being together that will make the friendship even stronger.

As with everything else in life, the key is figuring out what you want and what you're willing to do to get it—and then being honest about the results. Angelica and Clarence may get all, none, or part of what they want from their friends. The only comfort is that these issues tend to come up between friends anyway, whether smoking is an issue or not—and they seem to arise throughout one's life. Deciding what to do and how to handle all the feelings that come up is just one of those important life lessons that can turn out wonderfully, terribly, or some combination of the two.

If you *do* want to talk to a friend about smoking, here are some concrete suggestions. They're not guarantees of success, but they might make things go more smoothly.

- ***Pick an occasion to talk when both of you have plenty of time and neither of you is under a particular strain.*** Bringing up a sensitive topic when somebody has to leave in 10 minutes to go take a big test or just after someone has had a fight with a girlfriend or boyfriend is almost sure to go badly. If you're not sure whether you're picking a good time to talk, or if no good time ever seems to come up, let your friend know you've got something you'd like to discuss and work together to decide when to do it.
- ***Use "I" statements rather than "you" statements telling the other person what he/she has done.*** Which of these statements do you think is easier to hear: "You're just not the same person since you started smoking!" or "I feel left out because you don't seem to like any of the things we used to do together"? For most people, the second statement is more likely to be welcome because it doesn't place blame. "I" statements make you more vulnerable, but they're much more likely to encourage your friend to open up and be vulnerable too, or at the very least, to help you avoid an angry, offended response.
- ***Remember who you are and what you want.*** That one sounds simple, but it's harder than it sounds. When you're talking with someone you care about, it's easy to get pulled into his or her point of view. Staying clear about your own feelings and values will help you decide how you want to handle the conversation.
- ***Remember that your friend also has a point of view.*** Sometimes it's hard both to stay centered in your own values *and* to respect your friends' right to think differently. How much room in your friendship is there to disagree?

- ***Don't be afraid to call a time-out or suggest that you pick up the conversation another time.*** Sometimes, when you're talking about a sensitive topic, one or both people can only take so much at one time. Knowing when to take a break or call a week-long intermission can sometimes take the pressure off.
- ***Remember that you can make your own final decision later, after you've had time to process the conversation.*** Suppose you ask your friend if there's a way he or she can cut back on smoking in your presence, and your friend refuses point-blank. What do you do next? Insist on ending the friendship? Give in completely to keep your friend? Whatever you finally decide, you don't want to choose while feelings are running high. Keep in mind as you talk that you can make your own decisions later, when you've had time to cool off and sort things out.

Reaching Out to Family

Talking to family members can be both easier and harder than talking to friends. On the one hand, it's usually safer to fight or disagree with family members because you're more likely to believe the relationship won't end, even if you're both mad for a while. On the other hand, you usually have to live with your family for a long time, and not getting along can be intensely uncomfortable.

For both reasons, it's important to be thoughtful about what you do and don't want to bring up with family. See if you can distinguish between family issues that affect your life and those that simply get on your nerves. If your father thinks that no-smoking laws are stupid and you believe in them, that may be a disagreement you can live with. If he smokes in front of you and you worry about his health, or yours, you might feel more compelled to take action.

If you do decide to talk to family members about smoking, many of the suggestions we've made for reaching out to friends will help you talk to family members as well—especially the part about using "I" statements rather than blame-laying "you" statements. Here are a few other ideas that might make things go more smoothly.

- **Be prepared to compromise.** Compromise is probably the key to getting along with your family. Since neither they nor you are likely to leave for a while, finding a way to get along is especially important for both of you. That doesn't mean you should compromise on things that you feel are endangering your body, your safety, or your sense of self. But it does mean that for anything short of that, you might have to accept a little give and take.
- **Be persistent.** After all, just because you agreed to compromise today doesn't mean you can't come back and ask for a better deal next week, next month, or in three months. Vanessa might have to live with "no smoking on the second floor, but smoking at mealtimes" as her first compromise, but next month, she might be able to talk to either parent again about her feelings and concerns.
- **Be creative.** Lots of family battles get deadlocked because people become more concerned with winning than with finding a solution that will work for everyone. Maybe there are other ways to solve family problems that no one has ever thought of before. Maybe you'll be the one to come up with the new, workable idea. See what happens if you try to think of some new compromise, rather than staying locked in the same old battles.
- **Remember that if things get too tough, eventually, you can leave.** It's usually fairly hard for people to leave home before they've finished high school, but it gets a lot easier to leave after that. Even if secondhand

smoke or other smoke-related problems are driving you crazy, the bottom line is that someday, you'll be able to live in a house where *you* make the rules. And although it's not ideal to live in a cloud of secondhand smoke, the effects of that, too, are often reversible.

Smoking and Citizenship

If you've read the rest of this book, one of the things you've probably realized by now is how much people disagree about smoking. Even statements that most people in the public and private health communities agree upon—for example, "Smoking is hazardous to your health"; "Second-hand smoke causes cancer"; "Nicotine is addictive"—provoke some kind of response of disagreement from the tobacco industry, conservative policy institutes, and other observers. And within the public health community, there is a great deal of disagreement over what should be done to stop smoking, especially among young people, as well as over what should be done to protect people of all ages from secondhand smoke.

You are not just a potential smoker or nonsmoker; you are also a citizen. So part of your responsibility, through the teenage years and into adulthood, is not just to decide whether you personally want to smoke or not but also to think about what society's policy on smoking should be. Are you concerned with the rising rate of smoking among teenagers, or do you think that smoking is an individual decision that schools, government agencies, and other institutions should stay out of? Do you think that ads for smoking should be regulated, and if so, how? Or do you think that regulation of tobacco ads is too great a limit on free speech? What's your position on secondhand smoke? Should people be protected from it at work, at school, in restaurants, in other public places, or do smokers have a right to exercise their free choice?

Let's look for a moment at some of the ways that people have tried to address teen smoking. Here are some of the major responses that various public and private groups have tried or proposed in recent years.

- **Restrict advertising and promotion.** Some people argue that ads are the real culprits in the teen smoking story because they make smoking look so attractive. They're also concerned about the number of gifts with cigarette brand logos that tobacco companies send to teenagers. People who see advertising as a major factor in teenagers' decisions have argued for various positions, from banning cigarette ads in places where young people might see them, to restricting ads to black-and-white images or to text only. On the other hand, ad agencies, tobacco companies, the American Civil Liberties Union, and others have argued that advertising is part of our right to free speech and that all ideas—including the idea that smoking is fun—should be allowed into the public view.

- **Run counter-ads.** Some of the states that have won huge settlements from the tobacco industry have spent money on counter-advertisements, which try to put forth another view of smoking. Often, these counter-ad campaigns involve talking to young people, to get their views of what other teenagers might respond to. The MTV public service ads featuring Christy Turlington that we talked about in Chapter 5 are another example of using advertising to try to stop smoking, either specifically among teenagers or among people of all ages.

- **Increase legal penalties.** Many states and local communities are trying to crack down on stores that sell cigarettes to underage smokers and to get rid of or limit the use of vending machines, which young smokers can use more easily. Another legal approach is to increase the penalties against teenagers themselves, fining them heavily if they're caught smoking, or making them go to "smoking court," where they hear antismoking lectures from a judge. Others argue that focusing on *teenage* smoking simply makes cigarettes more attractive to young people, positioning them as something that only adults have access to. They contend that punishing young people for smoking will only make teens want to smoke more and that no matter what the penalties, young people will almost certainly be able to get their hands on cigarettes if they want them.

- ***Establish clean-air policies.*** Teenaged workers age 15–19 are the least likely to be protected by smoke-free workplace policies, and people of all ages are affected by clean indoor air policies. Americans for Nonsmokers' Rights and such notable figures as Professor Stanton Glantz (who received many of the tobacco company "secret documents") have argued that public policy should focus on changing conditions for teens and adults together, rather than singling teenagers out as some kind of "problem group."

What do *you* think? As a citizen who will someday be a voter, part of the decision you have to make about smoking is what you think your community and your society should do about it. In the next section, we'll make some final suggestions on ways you and your friends might take action.

Reaching Out to Your Community

All over the country, young people are taking various kinds of action on smoking—and other issues—in their communities. These kinds of activities usually don't get the press that more negative news about teenagers commands. Nevertheless it's true that young people can make a big difference in their world when they get organized.

If you and your friends would like to take action on smoking—at your school, in your neighborhood, or in your community—you might contact one of the groups listed in Chapter 7 to find out what others have done in your area or in other parts of the country. There are also several action guides listed in that chapter that you may want to consult. To get you started, here are a few specific suggestions.

- *Organize.* You've heard the expression, "Two heads are better than one." Well, when you're trying to solve a community problem, the more heads, the better. Get a group together and start talking about what *should* be done and what you *want* to do. You might be surprised at the ideas you come up with!
- *Brainstorm.* The first stage is to think of ideas—all sorts of ideas—about what might make your school or community a better place, or about the kinds of programs that would get people thinking about smoking in new and more helpful ways. Eventually, you can choose one idea to start with, but try to think big and then narrow your focus, rather than starting small. You might get further in the end.
- *Research.* If you're proposing a particular kind of rule or policy, find out if anyone else has ever tried it or if there is information that would affect the situation that you don't yet know about. If you're suggesting an educational program, such as a Smoking Awareness Day at your school, find out what speakers and other resources are available in your community. Again, the resources in Chapter 7 might be a good place to start. Your local library, hospital, school nurse, and guidance counselor might all be places to start.
- *Make a plan.* Here's where it's important to be realistic. Planning takes a lot of clear thinking and hard work, but it's what makes the difference between ideas that happen and ideas that stay ideas.

- ***Don't give up!*** Maybe your first or even your second, idea doesn't work. That's all right. Change can take years—or can happen overnight. The only way to make a difference is to keep plugging away at what you believe in. Again, the results can surprise you!

Finally, here's a quick list of some things teenagers in other communities have done. Do any of these appeal to you?

- ***Write letters***—to the school paper, the local paper, the city council, a particular employer.
- ***Meet with decision makers***—at the school board, a community board, a local government office.
- ***Create a public service announcement***—for radio or television.
- ***Start a Smoking Awareness Day at your school***—and maybe also get media attention for it.
- ***Try to get a local ordinance passed.***

As we've seen, smoking is a complicated issue. But it's one that affects every single one of us, through our individual choices to smoke or not smoke; via our exposure to secondhand smoke; in our economy; through the politicians, cultural groups, and educational institutions that are supported by tobacco industry money. Making choices about smoking—for yourself as an individual, for your community, for your society—is part of growing up. The more you know, the better choices you can make. Good luck!

7

Where to Find Help

Help with Quitting

The following organizations offer various types of help with quitting, as well as providing information on smoking and smoking-related diseases.

American Cancer Society
1599 Clifton Road NE
Atlanta, GA 30329
800-227-2345
http://www.cancer.org

American Heart Association
7272 Greenville Avenue
Dallas, TX 75231
214-373-6400

American Lung Association
1740 Broadway
New York, NY 10019
800-LUNG-USA
http://www.lungusa.org

Blair's Quitting Smoking Resources
www.quitsmokingsupport.com.
http://www.chriscor.com

Canadian Cancer Society
10 Alcorn Avenue, Suite 200
Toronto, Ontario M4V 3B1
Canada
416-961-7223
fax: 416-961-4189
http://www.cancer.ca/indexe.htm

Canadian Lung Association
888-566-LUNG (in Canada)
http://www.lung.ca/cla.html

Hazelden
15251 Pleasant Valley Road
PO Box 176
Center City, MN 55012-0176
800-328-9000

The Health Connection
55 West Oak Ridge Drive
Hagerstown, MD 21740
800-548-8700

National Cancer Institute
Publication Ordering Service
900 Rockville Pike

Bethesda, MD 20892
800-4-CANCER

Nicotine Anonymous World Services
2118 Greenwich Street
San Francisco, CA 94123

General Information

The following organizations and web sites can help you learn more about tobacco, smoking, and health, as well as the economic and political issues surrounding smoking, smokeless tobacco, and the tobacco industry. If the web site addresses change after press time, try typing in "teenage smoking" or some version of the organization's name on your search engine.

Action on Smoking and Health (ASH)
2013 H Street NW
Washington, DC 20006
202-659-4310
http://www.ash.org

American Lung Association
1150 Connecticut Avenue NW, Suite 820
Washington, DC 20036
202-452-1184

American Nonsmokers' Rights Foundations
2530 San Pablo Avenue, Suite J
Berkeley, CA 94702
510-841-3032
http://www.no-smoke.org/advo.html

Canadian Centre on Substance Abuse
75 Albert Street, Suite 300

Ottawa, Ontario K1P 5E7
Canada
613-235-4048
fax: 613-235-8101
http://www.ccsa.ca

Canadian Council for Tobacco Control (CCTC)
170 Laurier Avenue West, Suite 1000
Ottawa, Ontario K1P 5V5
Canada
613-567-3050
fax: 613-567-2730
http://www.cctc.ca/index.html

Centre for Health Promotion
University of Toronto
The Banting Institute
100 College Street, Room 207
Toronto, Ontario M5G 1L5
Canada
416-978-1809
fax: 416-971-1365
http://www.utoronto.ca/chp/

Cigarette Papers (tobacco company "secret documents")
http://www.library.ucsf.edu/tobacco

Coalition for Accountability
1225 I Street NW, Suite 350
Washington, DC 20005
fax: 202-789-1116
http://www.savelives.org

Corporate Watch
http://www.corpwatch.org

Essential Action
http://www.essential.org./action

Environmental Protection Agency
Indoor Air Quality Information Clearinghouse
PO Box 37133
Washington, DC 20013-7133
800-438-4318

Global Link—International Union Against Cancer
http://www.uicc.ch

National Center for Tobacco-Free Kids
1707 L Street NW, Suite 800
Washington, DC 20036
202-296-5469

N.O. P.A.T.S.Y
National Organization of People Attacking Tobacco Sales
to Youth
c/o Dr. Terry Polevoy
105 University Avenue East
Waterloo, Ontario N2J 2W1
Canada
http://www.healthwatcher.net/index-2.html

Operation S.C.A.T., Inc.
Student Coalition Against Tobacco
475 H Street NW
Washington, DC 20001

Physicians for a Smoke-Free Canada
PO Box 4849, Station E
Ottawa, Ontario K1S 5J1
Canada

613-233-4878
fax: 613-567-2730

STAMP: Stop Tobacco Access to Minors Project
55 Maria Drive, Suite 837
Petaluma, CA 94954
707-762-4591

STAT: Stop Teenage Addiction to Tobacco
121 Lyman Street, Suite 210
Springfield, MA 01103-9922
413-732-STAT
408-247-7828 (in San Jose, CA)

Mike Tacelosky
http://www.smokescreen.org

Tobacco Bulletin Boards, Gene Borio
http://www.tobacco.org

Tobacco Product Liability Project, Tobacco Control
Resource Center
http://www.tobacco.neu.edu

WAGAT: Women and Girls Against Tobacco
2001 Addison Street, Suite 200
Berkeley, CA 94704-1103
5100-841-6434

Washington DOC
http://www.kickbutt.org

Further Reading

Action Guides

These books will provide you with specific suggestions for taking action on smoking, as well as with general principles of ways to make change in your school and in your community.

Americans for Nonsmokers Rights. *How to Butt In: Teens Take Action Guidebook, or How to Make the Tobacco Industry Butt Out of Your Life!* Berkeley, Calif.: ASNR, 1995.

The Earthworks Group. *50 Simple Things You Can Do to Save the Earth.* Berkeley, Calif.: Earthworks Press, 1989.

————. *You Can Change America.* Berkeley, Calif.: Earthworks Press, 1993.

Hirschfelder, Arlene. *Kick Butts!: A Kid's Action Guide to a Tobacco-Free America.* New York: Simon & Schuster/Messner, 1998.

Lewis, Barbara. *The Kid's Guide to Social Action.* Minneapolis, Minn.: Free Spirit Publishing, 1991.

No Kidding Around! Kensington, Md.: Information USA, 1992.

General Information

Fahs, John. *Cigarette Confidential: The Unfiltered Truth About the Ultimate Addiction.* New York: Berkeley Books, 1996. The earlier part of the book includes an account of Fahs's personal struggle against an addiction to tobacco and a lively history of the tobacco industry in the United States. Later parts of the book include interviews he conducted with smokers and former smokers.

Glantz, Stanton A., John Slade, Lisa A. Bero, et al. *The Cigarette Papers.* Berkeley, Calif.: University of California Press, 1996. This volume contains the documents that created a national scandal: the "secret papers" suggesting that tobacco companies may have lied to Congress, manipulated the content of cigarettes, and deliberately targeted a youth market.

Hyde, Margaret O. *Know About Smoking,* New York: Walker, 1995. A good, basic introduction to issues about smoking, written in a style that is clear and easy to understand.

Krogh, David. *Smoking: The Artificial Passion.* New York: W.H. Freeman & Co., 1991. Krogh, a science writer, examines scientific studies of addiction to help readers understand just what it is that makes smoking so attractive and so difficult to give up. His last chapter contains suggestions for quitting.

Monroe, Judy. *Nicotine.* New York: Enslow, 1995. An overview of the effects of nicotine, the most chemically active ingredient in cigarettes and smokeless tobacco.

Tobacco: People, Profits & Public Health. Hudson, Wisc.: Gary McCuen Publications, 1997. An excellent collection of documents from a wide range of perspectives and disciplines. Information on science, politics, economics, civil liberties, the law, and other key issues, representing both antismokers and supporters of the tobacco industry.

Index

143